WHEN
KINGDOMS
CLASH

CINDY TRIMM

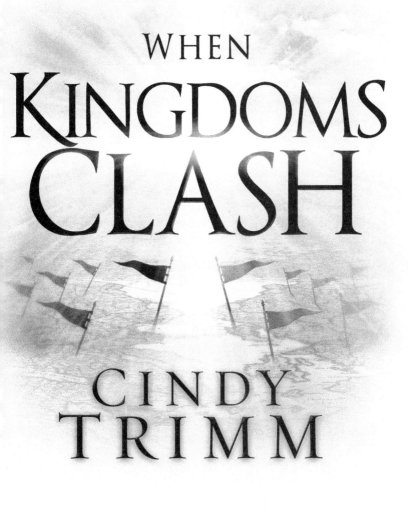

CHARISMA
HOUSE

Cover design by Justin Evans
Design Director: Bill Johnson
Manuscript preparation: Rick Killian, www.killiancreative.com

Visit the author's website at www.trimminternational.org.

Library of Congress Cataloging-in-Publication Data:
Trimm, Cindy.
  When kingdoms clash / Cindy Trimm. -- 1st ed.
     p. cm.
  Includes bibliographical references.
  ISBN 978-1-61638-948-2 (casebound) -- ISBN 978-1-62136-
014-8 (international trade pbk.) -- ISBN 978-1-61638-949-9
(ebook)
  1. Prayer--Christianity. I. Title.
  BV210.3.T77 2012
  248.3'2--dc23
                                      2012020415

CONTENTS

v

PROLOGUE

You meant evil against me; but God meant it for
good, in order to…save many people alive.
—GENESIS 50:20

I T GETS SURPRISINGLY cold in the desert at
night. There's no electricity, and oil lamps can
only just fight off the darkness; once they are out,
that darkness carries the cold right to your soul—
especially when you have nothing to lean against
except the stone walls of a jail cell.

Jo was a political prisoner in Egypt. He wasn't
there because of the recent uprisings but because
he had fallen into a power struggle between one of
the military leaders and the man's wife. As an aide
overseeing the affairs of the general's home and business interests, the general's wife had taken an interest
in Jo that was more than cursory. Amongst Egypt's
Desperate Housewives, bored in her pampered

lifestyle and neglected by her ambitious husband, she was attracted to Jo's youth, unflappable spirit and gift for making things prosper. If her husband wasn't working him so hard, he would have been a catch for any woman in Egypt, but instead he spent all his waking hours slaving away in her household and on their estate. She thought she could use his ambition to exploit what she wanted from him—a little afternoon distraction from her gilded cage—but it was not to be. It turned out that Jo had more character than ambition. He wasn't going to touch his boss's wife. When he rejected her advances, she told her husband he had tried to rape her and contrived to have Jo thrown into prison without a trial.

The years had not been kind to Jo overall, despite an auspicious beginning. He was born to a rich family in the north, but jealousy persuaded his brothers to try to kill him, and he had to flee for his life. Finding work with the general had first seemed like a godsend, but then even that turned against him, and he wound up in one of the poorest, dirtiest prison systems in the world, seemingly forsaken and forgotten.

But Jo wasn't alone.

Jo was a man of faith in the one true God. Although all he once had of wealth, position, and success was now stripped from him, Jo still had what he treasured most—his relationship with God. Rather than bemoan his horrible luck, he turned his hours of idle time to prayer. He prayed for his family who had abused him. He prayed for the government whose corrupt systems allowed for an innocent man to be locked up in prison for life without so much as a phone call to a lawyer. But most of all he prayed in pursuit of knowing God and His mysteries—of understanding the dream God had put into Jo's heart as a teenager. With nothing to call his own in the physical world, he sought spiritual treasure. As a result, God began to give him insight into dreams and visions. As he could, Jo helped other prisoners understand the messages from heaven God was trying to give them while they slept. Some were helped by it; others ignored his interpretations to their own demise.

For nearly half of his life now, Jo had been a fugitive and prisoner. Coming up on what should be the best days of his life, the cold stone on his back reminded him that the future held no promise of family or career for him. All he had was the moment he lived in—he had *now*. *Now* was all he may ever possess. So rather than despair, he invested his moments in eternity. God answered, not with prosperity, promotion, or deliverance as most would ask for, but with Himself. Not only did Jo find that comforting, but he also felt it was a greater blessing than being king of the world.

Jo clung to the stories of God his father had told him as a boy. He had no Bible to read, so he spent hours imagining the scenes of Abraham in the desert and Jacob wrestling with God. Despite his circumstances, he thought long and hard on the promises God had made to his father and his father's fathers before him, and what they might mean to him. Since he was in prison with no hope of ever getting out, he wondered if those promises belonged to him as much as them—but he knew if God could save Isaac from being sacrificed on the hilltop, God could intervene for him too. He also asked God about the dream in his heart almost every day—what had it meant? Was it still to come about? How was he going to go from inmate to being the leader he saw himself becoming? It seemed too much to imagine. Was it really possible he would go from the prison to the palace? What strange and wonderful set of events would have to happen to bring that about?

"Joseph!"

The voice pulled him from his prayerful thoughts, and suddenly the stone walls and bars were back. A shiver ran up his spine. He turned to the door and saw it was the warden.

"Sir?" Jo asked as if waking from sleep. "What on earth was the warden doing in the prison at this time of night?" he wondered.

"Joseph, the strangest thing has just happened. The president is calling for you. I am to have you washed, given new clothes, and in his counsel chambers within the hour."

"What?" Jo asked, wondering if he had dozed off and was dreaming. "How can that be?"

The warden unlocked the cell door and swung it open. "I don't know. I have never had anything like this happen before. But they seem to want something from you—something they think only you can do. I think this could be your break, Joseph! If you play this right, you could be getting out of here! I know that sounds impossible, but I think your God has just made a way for you. When you first came here, I doubted you. All your God talk and positive attitude stuff. I thought you were nuts, but then it just seemed like everything you touched improved. That really made me wonder. And now this. I wouldn't be surprised if you were going to get out of here—and I have to admit, it couldn't be happening to a better man."

Joseph looked up, out of the single window of his cell to the starry sky beyond. "So, bigger things, Lord?" he thought. "You always talked of other plans.

Is this what You meant? I never knew what to make of that."

Joseph paused as the warden opened the cell door. He closed his eyes for a moment in silent prayer. "You will go with me, won't You? I'd rather stay here than do something without You. Lord, if this is Your plan, I look forward to throwing myself into it—I want nothing else but to serve You! I can't wait to see what You are about to do next."

"Joseph?" the warden asked politely, giving him time to finish his prayer. "We mustn't keep him waiting. This way to see the president."

INTRODUCTION

We know that all things work together for
good to those who love God, to those who are
the called according to His purpose.
—ROMANS 8:28

THE PREVIOUS NARRATIVE is my imagining of the night Joseph was called before Pharaoh to interpret his dream. From the day he had been sold to the slavers by his brothers to the day he was called before Pharaoh, it had been more than thirteen years—thirteen years spent first as a slave and then as a convict. It would likely be another ten before he saw his family and the fulfilling of the dream God had shown him as a teenager. We tend to think about Joseph in his role as the prime minster of Egypt, directing the storing of grain and then using that to save the peoples of the Middle East during the greatest famine of his time. Or we think of Joseph in his robe of many colors, favored by his father above all of his other brothers. But we over-look Joseph in the pit, in the mud, waiting for his brothers to kill him; Joseph as a slave exiled from his life of wealth and favor; Joseph falsely accused by Potiphar's wife and thrown into prison without any hope of ever getting out; or Joseph, likely dressed in rags, emaciated with hunger, sitting in his cell one lonely desert night after another, seemingly alone and forsaken, but lost to the world in prayer.

But Joseph's is not a story of poverty and hard times. It is a story of triumph. It is a story of fiscal wisdom and insight that disciplined the management of resources so that Egypt not only survived the famine but also had enough to save the other nations of the Middle East, including the one that would one day become the nation of Israel. What had been meant to put him down and discourage him instead inspired the very character that delivered Joseph from poverty to prominence in one day.

If this was an isolated incident, we might be able to disregard it. But it is not. The Bible goes on to tell us of Moses, exiled into the desert and cast aside by his family, yet because he kept his heart in God's hands, one day God called him from obscurity to be the deliverer of his people from slavery. David was the runt of his family, not even called when Samuel came to his father, Jesse, looking to anoint the next king. And yet God took him from being an obscure shepherd to becoming king—and still much of the time in between he spent as an outlaw running for his life.

Gideon was hiding in a winepress; Ruth was gleaning at the edges of a field; Esther was kept locked away and preened for her husband's pleasures; John the Baptist was a homeless vagabond; Peter, a common laborer; Daniel, a kidnapping victim; Mary, a common village girl; Paul, a bloodthirsty bounty hunter. You don't have to look too hard to find someone worse off in these stories than you are now. No matter how low they started or how far they fell from grace, encountering God transformed them. Whether it was through their own prayers or those of someone else, they came face-to-face with God at some totally unexpected point in their lives, and they and their worlds were never the same again.

God specializes in turning lives around—no matter where we start or how little influence we may have had before, He gives us power to transform the world around us if we will but encounter Him and give ourselves to Him without holding anything back.

I know, because I started with nothing and

probably should never have amounted to anything. I was born into poverty in Bermuda into a family of seven children (I was the sixth). There were days we ran out of everything, including water. I know what it's like to have the odds against me—but I also know what it's like to start praying to the Father in heaven who loves me and have Him guide me out of the ghetto and into government. I never imagined as a young girl that I would be a senator.

In the case of Joseph, his entire young adulthood was taken from him, yet he lost no time. In fact, he actually finished ahead of the game. The difficulties the devil was using in an attempt to destroy Joseph's dreams he gave to prayer, and that prayer transformed Joseph from a self-centered brat into a man of wisdom and integrity who could rule a kingdom. The difference was not made overnight, even though his ascent from prison to prominence would be. The difference in Joseph was forged in the crucible of prayer, hour after hour, year after year. God became Joseph's most precious pursuit, his greatest desire, and his only hope. Turning his back on the world to seek God with all of his heart, Joseph was transformed into the man God would use to save a generation.

While these stories are millennia old, the principle

remains the same today. Martin Luther King Jr. was an obscure pastor before he became a man of national interest during the Montgomery, Alabama, bus boycott. Nelson Mandela spent decades in prison before he was released and eventually elected president of the very same nation that incarcerated him as a political prisoner. While he was in prison, what did he think about? What did he pray? What did he hold tightly to? We don't know completely, but we do know that during his twenty-seven years in prison he read the following poem every day:

Invictus

Out of the night that covers me,
Black as the Pit from pole to pole,
I thank whatever gods may be
For my unconquerable soul.

In the fell clutch of circumstance
I have not winced nor cried aloud.
Under the bludgeonings of chance
My head is bloody, but unbowed.

Beyond this place of wrath and tears
Looms but the Horror of the shade,
And yet the menace of the years
Finds, and shall find, me unafraid.

It matters not how strait the gate,
How charged with punishments the scroll,
I am the master of my fate:
I am the captain of my soul.
                    —WILLIAM EARNEST HENLEY

I don't share these stories because I love rags-to-riches tales, nor do I want you to put these men and women on some kind of pedestal. What I want you to see is they were just people—people like you or me—people in the worst of possible circumstances, in the most depressing of situations, with the most hopeless of outlooks, facing the greatest challenges of their times. But God didn't place them there to be defeated. He placed them there to be transformed into the fulcrums of cultural and moral revolution. Right in the darkest of places, when they sought Him with all of their hearts, God chose such men and women to become beacons for their nations, their industries, their generations, and their world.

Today they shine as lights showing what can happen when men and women refuse to compromise what is right to get along with what is wrong, and when they stand up for justice even though it could cost them everything. It shows how one person and God can form a majority. It shows how prayer not only changes us, but it also changes circumstances—and it not only changes circumstances, but it can also change hearts and minds for generations to come. The evil of a dictator or tyrant may reign for a few decades, but the good done by men and women of character and integrity influences centuries.

The front lines of the clash between the kingdoms of darkness and light do not usually happen in our churches; they happen where we live, where we work, and in what we do in our spare time. The battles take place in our workplaces, neighborhoods, where our children go to school, in our voting booths, and in the halls of influence. It may seem a little odd, but we cannot be the church we are called to be *in* our churches. Our churches should be places of equipping and coordinating, but then we have to take the fight to the streets.

To do that, we need to understand the importance of the practice and tactics of prayer as we never have before. We must pursue God as David did and trust in the dreams God has given us just as Joseph did, regardless of how our circumstances look.

In the previous two books of this series we went from battle plan to boot camp, and now it is time to engage the enemy in the field. In *The Art of War for Spiritual Battle* we looked at prayer from the prayer general's vantage point, exploring the nature of spiritual warfare and the overall tactics and strategies for engaging in it. In *The Prayer Warrior's Way* we looked at the requirements of being a soldier in the army of God and what disciplines are needed to fight effectively. In this book, *When Kingdoms Clash,* we will look at how to stay strong when the heat of battle is most intense and how to remain steady to see it through to victory.

There is a war going on. In every suburb, urban center, rural community, and nation on the earth there is a battle for the souls of our generation. In some places it is worse than others. It spans from mind-numbing song lyrics that glorify crime to body-mutilating sexual exploitations that condemn children and young people to an early grave. We see it in the pristine African savannahs where children are raised as pawns of war or where warlords rape and murder to keep millions on the edge of starvation—in nations where corruption keeps government inefficient and oppressive, to places where racial and ethnic hatred could explode into genocidal violence at any moment. At the same time this war is also in our own suburbs, cities, and rural communities. Domestic violence; recession;

sickness, disease, and disability; poverty; gang violence; and even lack of opportunity drive a deeper and deeper wedge between the haves and the have-nots, between the sexes, between mother and daughter, father and son, one form of faith and another, as well as each individual and their God-ordained destiny. Time and again people are failing to live the lives God put them on the earth to live—lives of fullness, abundance, understanding, acceptance, and joy. You don't have to dig too deeply into the headlines to see the array of injustices we must continue to stand against. We live in dark times, perhaps the morally darkest the world has ever experienced.

Yet when things are the darkest, even the smallest of lights can shine brightly enough for those who are lost to find their way out. Neither are we a people of little lights. Perhaps we should wash the words of that old childhood song "This Little Light of Mine" out of our memories. Jesus said it this way:

> You are the light of the world. *A city* that is set on a hill cannot be hidden. Nor do they light a lamp and put it under a basket, but on a lampstand, and it gives light to all who are in the house. Let your light so shine before

men, that they may see your good works and
glorify your Father in heaven.

—Matthew 5:14–16,
emphasis added

When Jesus talks of our light, He doesn't talk about
a candle first; He talks about a city. Why? Because
while you may have trouble seeing a single candle
from outer space, you can see a city from heaven.

We do indeed live in a time when there are horrible things happening on the earth, but we are not
powerless to change those things for the better. We
may balk at what we can accomplish because we do
not have authority or access in the halls of national
governments, but we forget that we have authority to
influence decisions made in the council chambers of
the very Creator of the universe Himself. We have
influence. We are change agents. We have authority
in the heavenlies. We are, in fact, the keys to making
a difference for thousands if not millions. We do it
through the atomic power of prayer. But if we don't
understand our positions and power in our places
of prayer, we will make no difference at all. It's like
picking up a bugle when we don't know how to play
it. We can certainly get attention from making noise
with it, but we exercise no skill and command no

authority with the noises we make. No one is going to gather at the sound of our call to battle or discern heaven's strategic commands to move in unison. It is like arguing a case before a jury while not speaking the language of the courtroom. For all of our enthusiasm, we will do no good.

It's time to turn our eyes away from our circumstances and to the God who called Joseph from the prison cell, Moses from the desert, David from the fields, Peter from his fishing boat, and Paul from his terrorism. Wherever you are in space and time is the place God has placed you to see what you see and be concerned about what you are concerned about. Chances are, what bothers you also bothers God. You are His agent, wherever you are, to make things different.

We live in a world characterized by wars and rumors of war. We are in the heat of battle—warring for our children, fighting for our marriages, our homes, our health, our job security, and our nation. At a national and global level there is a war on drugs, terrorism, hunger, and slavery. Battles are raging and the stakes are high, but only when our actions are saturated by prayer will we see breakthrough and victory.

Prayer is the strongest problem-solving power available to humanity. S. D. Gordon said, "The greatest thing that anyone can do for God and man is to pray. Prayer is the winning blow." Prayer is dynamic. Prayer is a kingdom technology and spiritual weapon of mass destruction against evil. In the natural, technology is the actual application of scientific methodologies, especially to systemic, industrial, or commercial objectives. Prayer is the application of heaven's methodologies that systematically brings to pass God's plan for man. Prayer is a spiritual force that exerts and exercises continuous and decisive influence on both the natural and spiritual worlds, effecting change within its systems and inhabitants. Therefore prayer should be the salient feature of every believer's life strategy. Without it we are doomed. With it we are more than a conqueror.

✤ PART ONE ✤

PRAYER *From the* STRONGHOLD

To men [and women] who think praying their main business and devote time to it according to this high estimate of its importance does God commit the keys to his kingdom, and by them does he work his spiritual wonders in this world. Great praying is the sign and seal of God's great leaders and the earnest of the conquering forces with which God will crown their labors.[1]

—E. M. Bounds

One

RIGHT WHERE YOU ARE

Understanding Our Purpose in Prayer

> The church, you see, is not peripheral to the world;
> the world is peripheral to the church. The church
> is Christ's body, in which he speaks and acts, by
> which he fills everything with his presence.
> —EPHESIANS 1:22–23,
> THE MESSAGE

S O WHEN GOD calls, will He find you ready for your mission on the earth?

When God came to Joseph as a teenager in a dream, He came to a proud, headstrong young man who didn't have the discretion to keep his message from God to Himself. What was meant as a launching point into a life of civil service instead became a lightning rod for his brothers' jealousies and the catalyst for his being sold into slavery. I can't help believing that had Joseph's heart been different

15

at that point in in life, his trek from his father's estates in Canaan to leadership in Egypt might have been completely different. What might have happened had Moses not taken it into his own hands to try to deliver the Hebrew slaves as a younger man and never killed that Egyptian? Might their journeys have been more like David's or Daniel's? Journeys that started with hearts devoted to God rather than needing major course corrections and years lost in the wilderness before God could come to them again and reintroduce them to their purposes?

Where will you be when God comes to you with His greater plan for your life? Will you be open to step into it, or will you need to be schooled on the backside of the desert as Moses was, or will you need to go through a humbling process as rigorous as Joseph's? The difference will be determined by your prayer life—one way or the other.

When God found Saul (who would become Paul) on the road to Damascus, He found a man full of religion and knowledgeable in the Scriptures but ignorant of who God really was. Saul was so zealous for "righteousness," he was willing to instigate murder to protect religion as he knew it. But ultimate truth is not found in religion; it is found in Jesus. Certainly we can learn from religion as a way of pursuing God, but we must come to Jesus to truly understand God. Paul could have wasted his entire life trying to please God in his own way, but when he met Jesus, everything changed. Paul turned his zeal to prove himself into becoming a man of prayer hungry to know Jesus through the Spirit and the Word. Because Paul sought Jesus with such intensity, it was to Paul that God revealed the architecture of the church, and not one of the other apostles. This is why Paul was the primary writer inspired by God to pen the New Testament.

What changed in Paul? We read it in Acts 9, immediately after he encounters Jesus on the road to Damascus: "He was three days without sight, and neither ate nor drank" (v. 9). Though it doesn't say it directly here, I can't believe Paul only fasted during this period. I believe for the first time in his life he also began to truly humble himself and seek God. In Galatians he adds, "I did not immediately confer with flesh and blood" (Gal. 1:16), inferring that his initial years as a Christian were not in being taught by the disciples, but being taught by Christ Himself through prayer.

Though it is possible Paul may have heard Jesus speak in person, there is no historical record of it. I think Paul would never have been the persecutor he became had he ever met Jesus in the flesh. And because he was the only early apostle who didn't know Jesus as a human being, his role became a foundational one. Like those who would follow in the centuries to come who could not walk with Jesus as Peter, John, and the rest of the disciples had done, Paul would be the apostle who best understood the nature of the church—the fellowship of all the people to come who could only know Jesus through prayer and the Bible.

Though meeting Jesus face-to-face on the road to Damascus changed the direction of Paul's life forever, it was no overnight transformation. It would take roughly seventeen years of prayer and study for him to become the man we know as Paul, the apostle to the Gentiles. (See Galatians 1:18–2:1.)

Thus we see two distinct events occurring in the lives of all of these Bible heroes. There was a point of calling and a point of launching into that calling, or what many have labeled being *called* and then *separated* as outlined in Acts 13:2: "Now *separate* to Me Barnabas and Saul for the work to which I have called them" (emphasis added). Paul had been called to the work of God since before he was born—"God, who had set me apart even from my mother's womb and called me through His grace" (Gal. 1:15, NAS)—but he would not be separated into that calling until God saw that he was ready to be the man capable of walking in that calling. We see there is always a time of preparation of which intimate, consistent prayer is a major component. For Paul, as it had been for Joseph, that preparation happened after the first major revelation from God (Joseph's dream as a teenager vs. Paul's encounter with Jesus on the road to Damascus), while for others like Daniel and David, that preparation in prayer would happen before their initial callings were recognized (when David was anointed by Samuel and when Daniel was called before Nebuchadnezzar to interpret his dream); those times of recognizing the calling and being separated happened almost simultaneously.

"CALLED-OUT" ONES

The word for *church* in the New Testament is the Greek word ἐκκλησία, which can literally be translated as "the called out." If someone is called out of something, someone else must be doing the calling. In this sense the word ἐκκλησία has the connotation of being an assembly of those called out by a king to hear his vision for how his kingdom should be. More specifically, each person in the assembly has a unique calling or responsibility to fulfill in that kingdom, a place and a job no other member of the group can fill. With the world in its current state, every individual who confesses Jesus Christ as Savior and Lord should at some point arrive at a place of seeking, understanding, and conforming to the unique calling God has for him or her. This is the first, and therefore the most important, purpose of prayer. We can know about salvation and many other important components of living in the kingdom of God through the preaching of the Word, but God's individual plan for each life can only be revealed and confirmed by those who seek Him in Spirit and in truth.

The church is an assembly of individuals at various stages of preparation—between those who are just coming in response to God's calling them to Himself, and those who are already separated into the mission God has for them on the earth. While this should be a continuum evenly spread out from one end to the other, it has been my experience that our modern churches tend to be heavy on the calling end and increasingly lighter as we move toward those who are "separated" into what God has called them to do on the earth. We get saved and join the church, but too often after that we don't do much more than fill the pews every Sunday morning and Wednesday night.

I believe there are a number of reasons for this. Now it would be easy at this point to wander into the problems that, over the centuries, have worked to make the church less than what God intends it to be. While there might be some lessons worth learning in that discussion, it is much more than we have space for here and would not profit us enough to make it worth the digression. Most contemporary churches, I believe, are interested in what the Spirit of God is saying today and learning how they can get in step with the Holy Spirit to see Him work more among their members and in their communities. So rather than look for blame, I think it is better to look for practices that can take us into more fully being the church God wants on the earth rather than exploring all of the reasons for our shortcomings.

So, practically speaking, as the local church fights to keep the gospel of Jesus Christ at the forefront, it is often difficult to take our energies away from evangelism to establishing the kingdom of God in our communities. Most active churches today spend most of their time on the gateway doctrines of how to become a follower of Jesus. Helping people make the decision to follow Christ has become our *raison d'être*—our *reason to be*. We have worked so long and hard to get people to make that one decision we have forgotten the riches entire societies experience when we establish His kingdom on earth.

This has caused a gradual splitting of the Christian persona. Late in the 1800s organizations such as The Salvation Army under the leadership of William and Catherine Booth and George Müller's children's homes saw taking care of the poor and needy, the orphans and the widows, the oppressed and the exploited, as the main duty of the church. They worked hard for social reformation and started many of the institutions we think of today as being the responsibility of the government: unemployment bureaus, job training, shelters for the homeless, housing for orphans, distribution of welfare, and so forth. Their theology was based on the idea that the world would get better and better as the kingdom of God expanded to the extent that things would be so good on earth Jesus could simply take over. Schools taught from the Bible—many reading primers were based on biblical principles, ethics, and passages—and students opened each morning in prayer. (The Pledge of Allegiance wasn't heard in schools until the 1940s.) Prohibition, in fact, was a major triumph of this kind of thinking (and despite how most historians portray prohibition, it did a great deal for changing the view of drinking alcohol in the United States and greatly diminished the abuse of hard alcohol even after it was repealed). Think for a moment what it took to mobilize an entire nation to introduce a constitutional amendment to prohibit the sale of alcoholic beverages of any kind, and you will begin to understand how much influence these Christian groups marshaled at the turn of the twentieth century.

But things began to change in the early 1900s. With the failure of Prohibition and then the Scopes trial in 1925 that brought questions of God's creation of the universe into public debate, Christians began to slowly see "the world" as a dangerous place—and almost systematically began separating into their own subculture. People began to see a divide between what they did "at church" and what they did the rest of the week. This met its height when prayer was finally removed from the schools in 1962. Children began learning one set of rules for the classroom and lunchroom, and another set in Sunday school and at the family dinner table. As towns and cities grew larger and less connected, they also learned that they were less and less likely to be held accountable on Sunday morning for what they did on Saturday night. The rift in their own lives and in society between the secular and the sacred became increasingly greater. The Christian paradigm shifted from establishing the kingdom of heaven on earth to preserving oneself and loved ones from the world for heaven's sake.

Our methods for helping the poor and the lowly went from unleashing the kingdom of heaven into the world—remember what Jesus said His mission was in Isaiah 61 and Luke 4:18–19—"saving people's souls." Suddenly undoing conditions that fed poverty, neglect, and exploitation became secondary to saving the poor, neglected, and exploited spiritually. Doing what we could to put a Band-Aid on their physical needs, we pushed on to save the soul of someone else. We began living for heaven and becoming of less and less earthly good.

But the Great Commission of Matthew 28:18–20 did not tell us to make converts—it says we are to "make disciples." The local church was to be more than a mailing list and a place to hold choir practice. It is heaven's consulate on foreign soil. It is an educational center, a gathering place for the most creative and caring minds in a community to meet and brainstorm solutions and celebrate successes. It is where people come to meet people representing heaven—ambassadors and aid workers—to negotiate how to get their needs met physically, socially, emotionally, intellectually, and spiritually. The church is the microcosm of the kingdom of God on earth. When people walk into a local church, they should be getting a feel for what it would be like to step into the kingdom of heaven. Because of this, the church only finds its expression when its context is the kingdom of God. If we are living in anything less, we are walking in frustration and defeat.

The concept of the church was originated by Jesus. It did not exist in the Old Testament. Its function is different from that of the tabernacle. The tabernacle was the place where the holy of holies was kept and the presence of God dwelt among His people. Men and women would come to the tabernacle, but they couldn't go into the presence of God. The church, however, is for the body of Christ to gather in God's presence and in whom the Holy Spirit dwells. In the New Testament the tabernacle is compared to the body of the individual believer within whom God is present: "Do you not know that your body is the temple of the Holy Spirit who is in you?" (1 Cor. 6:19). The head of the church, Jesus Himself, was to have communication directly with each individual part of the body, but body parts don't function well without each other. Digestive organs don't have much worth without coordinating their activities with the hands that put food into the mouth. Feet don't have much purpose without eyes and ears to help them know where to run. Without the body, Christ the head has no vehicle to put into action His thoughts,

His concepts, His ideologies, His insights, His precepts, His philosophies, or His strategies. He prophetically speaks these things into the atmosphere of the church—into the "bubble" of His presence that is His body on the earth—looking for those who will listen and put His plans into operation. But each of us holds only a part of the "mystery" of God's plan for the earth. We need each other to get the whole picture. Thus the church is not a building; it is a collection of all those who hear and obey God's voice. It is the compilation and integration of all those who know how to pray, use prayer to hear from heaven, and then look for ways to make what they hear a reality on the earth.

In Ephesians 3:9 Paul called the church "the fellowship of the mystery," or you could say, of those who have "insight into the mystery of Christ" (Eph. 3:4, NAS). In the New American Standard translation of Ephesians 3:9 Paul calls it "the administration of the mystery." What is the purpose of this "fellowship" or "administration"? As Paul describes it, grace was given:

> To the intent that now the manifold wisdom
> of God might be *made known by the church*
> to the principalities and powers in the heavenly places, according to the eternal purpose

> which He accomplished in Christ Jesus our
> Lord, in whom we have boldness and access
> with confidence through faith in Him.
> —EPHESIANS 3:10–12,
> EMPHASIS ADDED

This means that even the angels in heaven are waiting to understand the mystery of God's plan of the ages for our universe—and that they won't learn it from going to God and asking; they can only learn it by watching the church on the earth and seeing God's mysterious plan revealed through us. As Paul stated earlier in Ephesians, God has "made known to us the mystery of His will, according to His good pleasure" (Eph. 1:9). That is quite a responsibility and quite a privilege at the same time. And somehow I think it is a whole lot more than just adding names to our list of people whose souls got saved through our ministries. God has bigger mysteries to reveal to the world. He still has "greater works" (John 14:12) to be done.

THIN PLACES

Paul was thoroughly Roman. It is hard not to see his Greco-Roman way of expressing ideas and his integration of Greco-Roman philosophies in what he taught and wrote. It is only natural. To reach the

Romans, he spoke as a Roman; to reach the Jews, he spoke as a Jew. As he described it, "I have become all things to all men, that I might by all means save some" (1 Cor. 9:22). Paul made it a point to learn how each different culture interacted with God that he might better be able to open up the mystery of Christ to that group. As different cultures interacted with the Word of God, he found each understood nuances that were different from any other culture, and I am sure Paul learned from each culture's different interactions with Christ.

That is one of the reasons I am fascinated to see how different societies and groups come to understand Jesus when they meet Him, no matter what their former religion or background. I believe that in every religion on the earth there are seeds of truth for understanding God—for if a religion held no truth at all, I don't believe anyone would follow it. And though Jesus is the only door through which we can come to God, I think there are nuances of knowing God that each holds uniquely. As I like to say it, there are many roads but only one door. Western culture will never understand all there is to know about God unless it listens to how other cultures and ethnicities come to God through Christ. We are the body, not the brain— we each only "know in part" (1 Cor. 13:12). This is why I found such revelation for prayer in looking at the ancient writings of Sun Tzu's *The Art of War*— because of his Eastern heritage, he brought things to the conversation of warfare and prayer I never would have encountered on my own.

I believe a similar thing happened when the first missionary went outside of the Roman Empire to preach the gospel of Jesus Christ. This missionary was not Paul, who only went to places within the Roman Empire, but Patrick, who went to the Celts sometime around A.D. 432 when the influence of Rome was waning. The Roman church followed Roman ways. It established itself in the centers of power, building its churches where garrisons established strongholds, and then ministering to the people as they came to these local capitals. However, when the gospel interacted with the Celtic culture, things were done differently. Instead, Celtic ministers went out to where the people were. They built their churches and monasteries in the town squares, the markets, and at the most traveled crossroads. And there they prayed and served the communities. They became scribes because people needed books to keep their traditions, and some even credit the Irish with saving Western culture, for if it had not been for these scribes, we might not have the works of

Plato, Aristotle, Homer, Virgil, and the like for our libraries today. All the copies would have been lost as Rome disintegrated.*

In going into these places looking to serve, they didn't come with ruling armies. By nature the friars emerged from the tradition of Celtic warriors, fighters who were fearless to the point of appearing insane to their enemies. The friars were, in essence, warrior-monks. When they came to serve, they also came to fight, but understanding spiritual things, they fought their battles in the heavenlies first and foremost. They came to places, looked around, started praying, and then did what God told them in prayer to do.

The areas bathed in this kind of prayer received a reputation as "thin places," places where the veil between heaven and earth had been so worn by prayer that it was easier for things to get "through." I can't think of a better, simpler definition of the purpose of prayer and what the church is for. We are to be the places where heaven touches earth—where the laws and provision of the kingdom of heaven are most readily available.

Our churches aren't to be as much rescue centers as they are to be embassies representing God's kingdom

---

* See Thomas Cahill's *How the Irish Saved Civilization*.

here on the earth. They are to be cultural exchange centers that bring different backgrounds and religions together to meet Jesus and see what they can learn at the foot of the cross and the mouth of the empty tomb. They are to be centers for creativity, art, expression, innovation, invention, and transformation. They are to be places where half ideas meet one another to become whole; where hunches bump into each other to inform solutions; where diversity begets new levels of understanding, revelation, and insight; where pieces of the great puzzle of the mystery of Jesus Christ can find one another and connect. They are to be educational centers helping people to learn the paradigm of heaven and how to see as God sees. We enter and join our local churches as people seeking citizenship in a new kingdom, but we should leave equipped to be ambassadors and representatives of that kingdom in our workplaces, neighborhoods, and even our own homes. Instead we tend to sneak out like spies hoping not to get caught—this ought not to be!

The true point of education is not to conform people into an image that someone has of what the proper "citizen" of a community should look like, but to pull out of each person—to reveal, uncover, discover, unearth, mine, expose, and then equip, nurture, refine, develop, and unleash—what God placed within that individual before the day she or he was born, the very thing the world needed that it never had before. The world system understands that if you can control the educational system, you can control people's belief systems, and that if you can control a person's belief system, you can control his or her destiny. The church needs to get a handle on that as well. We are not here to control people and have them join and support our rosters; we are to unleash the little bit of the kingdom of God locked up within each of them and let it loose on the world!

Destiny is God-given, God-revealed, and God-directed, or it is nothing. This is why we, the church, must renew our vigor and discipline in prayer. We must understand it anew. We have a world to transform, and we need God ideas to do it. The only way to get those will be to once again wear thin the veil between heaven and earth through prayer. We each have a part to play. We each have giftings, callings, abilities, skills, and talents God has uniquely given us to impact our jobs, communities, nations, and world. It is time to bring those to the battlefronts and start pushing the enemies back into the sea. It is time for more of us to stand up and take our places in the fight.

Two

BATTLE STATIONS!

Understanding Our Place in Prayer

God does nothing but in answer to prayer....Every new
victory which a soul gains is the effect of a new prayer.
—JOHN WESLEY

THE MAN OF God stood on an outcropping of
rocks on the side of the mountain addressing
a crowd that spanned into the distance. "How
long will you falter between two opinions?" he cried.

All the able-bodied of Israel who could come had
gathered at the prophet's invitation for a showdown
between the kingdom of Ahab and the kingdom of
Jehovah. On Elijah's cleft of rock he stood alone; on
another opposing him stood 450 of Baal and 400
prophets of the grove who had come at Ahab's command and represented his gods. The odds were over-
whelmingly lopsided to the natural eye, but Elijah

seemed unimpressed by the multitude he faced. Many in the crowd sensed they would see blood that day. It would be Elijah's last day to trouble Israel. Some took bets on it. Others secretly prayed to the true God of Israel for His prophet's deliverance—they prayed under their breath, afraid someone in the crowd next to them might see their lips moving and call them out.

"If the LORD is God, follow Him; but if Baal, follow him."

At this, even the gamblers grew silent and looked to the man standing alone. Such brashness! Such bravado! Such defiance of the king! Surely he would be struck down that day—but what if, just on the slightest chance, there was something more behind his bold words than deluded arrogance? What if, just by chance, the God of their fathers was the one true God and they were the ones who had been fooled? What if there was another way to live? What if there was a better way of justice? Would this Elijah really show it to them? Or would he die a bloody death right before their eyes?

The tension in the air was palpable. Did God really exist?

Then Elijah laid out the plans for a duel between two kingdoms—Baal versus Jehovah. Two bulls would be laid out and prepared for sacrifice on a platform of wood, but they would not light the fire. The prophets of Baal would call on the name of their god, and Elijah would call on the name of the Lord. Elijah looked over the crowd intently and ended the challenge with, "And the God who answers by fire, He is God."

The people answered, "It is well spoken."

Elijah let the prophets of Baal go first. It was early morning as they started, and then hour followed hour of them calling out in prayer. They grew increasingly more agitated as the time dragged on. They began dancing around the altar, leaping like mad men.

Around noontime the crowd had grown bored with the performance and was sitting in groups eating lunch and talking, only looking up from time to time to see if anything had changed. Suddenly Elijah spoke again. "Cry aloud, for he is a god; either he is meditating, or he is busy, or he is on a journey, or perhaps he is sleeping and must be awakened." Pricked by his words, the prophets of Baal became all that much more agitated and even brought out knives and cut themselves to sprinkle their blood on the altar as they cried out for fire. The crowd grew silent and enthralled again as blood gushed from the prophets of Baal, but still nothing. Hours later they had grown bored with the show again and went back to talking among themselves.

As the time of the evening sacrifice passed, Elijah felt he had given them enough time. "Come near to me," he called out to the people—and the crowd that remained rose up and gathered closer. The tension grew. Before him was an ancient altar that had been forgotten and left to the elements for generations. Elijah took one stone and piled it upon another, twelve stones in all—one for each tribe of the nation of Israel. The reverence with which he did this was nothing anyone in the crowd had seen before. They pressed in to see what was happening, awed by a change in the atmosphere like nothing they had ever felt. It was frightening and comforting at the same time; glorious and awe-filled all at once.

Elijah had trenches dug around the altar. Then he piled on the wood, prepared the bull, and laid it out on the wood. "Fill four waterpots with water, and pour it on the burnt sacrifice and on the wood," he commanded. It was done. "Do it a second time," he called out. Again, it was done. "Do it a third time," he ordered, and he was obeyed.

The trough was full of water, the wood drenched and dripping, the meat soaked. If you had covered it with oil and set a torch to it, the oil might have caught fire, but it would have soon burned out without so much as evaporating all of the water. The crowd was perplexed and baffled by these actions. What could Elijah possibly be planning to do?

Then Elijah lifted his eyes to the heavens and prayed:

> LORD God of Abraham, Isaac, and Israel, let it be known this day that You are God in Israel and I am Your servant, and that I have done all these things at Your word. Hear me, O LORD, hear me, that this people may know that You are the LORD God, and that You have turned their hearts back to You again.

Immediately, like a thunderbolt, fire fell from heaven, consuming the sacrifice, the wood, the stones of the altar, and instantly evaporating all the water in the trenches. In seconds, there was nothing left but scorched, steaming earth.

The crowd fell to their faces and cried out, "The LORD, He is God! The LORD, He is God!"[1]

When you pray, take courage, because you serve the God who answers by fire.

FALTERING BETWEEN TWO OPINIONS

Sometimes we forget we live in enemy territory.

For us as Christians, this world is not our home.

The day we chose to become followers of Jesus Christ, we rejected the confines, authority, and customs of this earthly kingdom in favor of the freedom, power, and lifestyle of heaven. The trouble is, while we were spiritually renewed and reconnected with the kingdom of God, physically we didn't translate from one realm to the other. We are not suddenly absent in the flesh and present with the Lord. We have been transformed from being natives of the earth to tourists—but more than that, we have changed our allegiance from being a loyalist to a resistance fighter. We are now part of God's freedom fighters. We no longer support the power structure of a corrupt government that preys upon its citizens, but we have become agents of change, looking for opportunities to oust the current despot—the one 2 Corinthians 4:4 calls "the god of this world" (NAS)—countering his propaganda and recruiting new members to join us in the fight. We seek to free the prisoners, open the eyes of the blind, bring good news to the impoverished, and bind up the wounds of the broken and oppressed. We are God's dissidents, and though our activities are not always secretive and classified, we are not welcome members of the one "world party." Some even scorn our activities as subversive and conspiratorial—and indeed, if we are truly doing our jobs as God's agents on the earth, they are, but they also have a completely different aim. We aren't "selling something" or trying to get someone to buy into our ideologies so we can control them or take advantage of their support—we are looking to set people free in Christ, the only true freedom that exists on the earth.

You see, we are not here to live in peace with evil and tolerate an oppressive regime—we are here to throw the powers that be out of high office and establish our God's rule there instead. Those powers and principalities that rule the atmosphere of this world and poison it with lies, deceptions, jealousies, lust, infidelity, profanity, depravity, vice, manipulation, racism, bigotry, contentiousness, outbursts of rage, selfish ambition, power mongering, cliquishness and divisiveness, abuse, drunkenness, addictions, gluttony, arrogance, and the like have no patience for the practitioners of "love, joy, peace, longsuffering, kindness, goodness, faithfulness, gentleness, self-control" (Gal. 5:22–23). We in turn should have no patience at all for them. Those things that strive to steal life from our children, neighbors, and loved ones should not be allowed any foothold in our jurisdictions.

But such authority and freedom are not won without a fight. And the thing is, the fight has already been won for us spiritually speaking, but we must manifest it naturally. The enemy is already defeated. When we deal with devils and demons now, we are dealing with con artists, charlatans who deceive like master magicians. The only authority they have is what they can trick or intimidate people out of. That's why Satan works so hard to spread his propaganda of fear and deception in our music, movies, and media, voice-printing our minds in order to create mental strongholds and paradigms. He wants to strangle the voices of our consciences and harden our hearts to the humanity of others. He has no right to still be in charge, but like syndicated crime, he ekes out control by bullying, corrupting, threatening, scaring, and preying on the basest desires of human beings. Those motivated by greed, lust, or envy are as easy to manipulate as those high on drugs—their addiction to the pride of life and other lusts of the flesh may not be as easy to recognize, but they render them as vulnerable to destruction.

If we never realize the authority God has given us, the enemy has no reason to relinquish his. He is a criminal who takes what doesn't belong to him and commands those he has no authority over. Jesus won the victory, but He is not here on earth to enforce it—He has entrusted that to us, His body.

Have you ever seen a head try to do something

without its body? That sounds like one of those old, second-rate science fiction movies where some guy's brain is hooked into a supercomputer to run a city. It never works. Heads only do well if their bodies stay connected to them, and bodies only succeed when they are connected and obedient to the head. If you don't believe me, try to have your head go to work without your body (or vice versa) and see how it turns out. Life just doesn't work that way.

Few ever stop to realize that heaven depends as much, if not more, on us as Christians than we as Christians do on heaven. The Bible tells us that in Christ "we live and move and have our being" (Acts 17:28), but it also tells us:

> So I sought for a man among them who would make a wall, and stand in the gap before Me on behalf of the land, that I should not destroy it; but I found no one.
>
> —EZEKIEL 22:30

Within our generation, there is a need for us to respond to this challenge by stepping out from the shadows of timidity into the spotlight of moral and ethical leadership. There is a place for each of us in the fight between goodness and darkness on this planet. If we don't stand in our places on the battle lines, there will be gaps in our defenses, and all the authority of heaven will mean very little. Unexercised or unrealized authority is no authority at all. As Archimedes said, "Give me the place to stand, and I will move the earth." Leadership, like the lever of Archimedes, when placed on the fulcrum of prayer, empowers individuals to make positive changes within their lives and communities, thereby altering the course/trajectory of nations and moving the world and humanity towards a better quality of life for all. In the spirit we are the same: we need the right place to stand and apply God's Word in order to overturn the systems and syndicates that would keep our generation enslaved, impoverished, and subjugated.

When Jesus came to the earth and announced His mission on the earth, He quoted Isaiah 61. As it is recorded in Luke, He announced:

> "The Spirit of the LORD is upon Me,
> Because He has anointed Me
> To preach the gospel to the poor;
> He has sent Me to heal the brokenhearted,
> To proclaim liberty to the captives
> And recovery of sight to the blind,

To set at liberty those who are oppressed;
To proclaim the acceptable year of the Lord."

Then He closed the book, and gave it back
to the attendant and sat down. And the eyes
of all who were in the synagogue were fixed on
Him. And He began to say to them, "Today
this Scripture is fulfilled in your hearing."
—Luke 4:18–21

It's time for us to find our footing and start pushing
back for the things Jesus came to this earth to deliver.

Taking Your Stand

When soldiers and warriors are taught to fight,
whether it be martial arts, boxing, or how to shoot a
gun, one of the first things they are taught is how to
stand. The proper stance is crucial to keeping your
balance in an attack as well as supporting the power
of your strikes against our enemy. If you have ever
watched a sumo wrestling match, you will notice
that most of the battle is about the preparation of
the stance—the fight itself is relatively short. The
one with the most solid stance is always the winner;
the one thrown off-balance always loses. The same
principle applies in the spiritual realm and in prayer.

Courage is the resolve to do something or become

something in spite of fear, hardship, obstacles, and opposition. Courage allows you to accept your fear, embrace it as a legitimate emotion, and use it as fuel to accomplish specific goals. Fear is an irrational emotion that accompanies you as you move from the familiarity of your comfort zone into new and unknown territories. Ambrose Redmoon said, "Courage is not the absence of fear, but rather the judgment that something else is more important than fear."

The courage that overcomes all fear is the courage that is born of God, who places a divine overcoming, courageous gene within you by His Spirit. He has not given you the spirit of fear (2 Tim. 1:7). Look deeply within, and you will find the courage to step forward and take a stand. The Bible tells us in 1 John 4:4, "You belong to God....You have already won a victory...because the Spirit who lives in you is greater than the spirit who lives in the world" (NLT). It is manifested when you develop a healthy, realistic perspective of who you are in God and when you realize what He has wired you to do and to become. Many people have become a slave to unfounded fear. Unfounded fear is a peculiar state of dis-ease within the imagination, arising largely out of a lack of knowledge. The Bible states that we perish because we lack knowledge (Hosea 4:6). I believe that not only do we dwindle away and die carrying seeds of greatness, unrealized potential, unpublished best sellers, unsung melodies, undiscovered medical breakthroughs, unfinished groundbreaking theories and philosophies, unmanifested multibillion-dollar inventions, and unestablished global business with us to the grave, but also our lack of knowledge causes divine opportunities and strategic relationships to die along with them.

When you become a slave to unfounded fear, you also become a slave to faulty beliefs, nonproductive behaviors, self-defeating paradigms, maladaptive practices, and ineffective and inappropriate responses that are inconsistent with your desire for well-being, success, and prosperity. So it is a matter of necessity that you understand the importance of courage and the benefits associated with its application to all facets of your life.

General Matthew B. Ridgway said, "There are two kinds of courage, physical and moral, and he who would be a true leader must have both. Both are the products of the character-forming process, of the development of self-control, self-discipline, physical endurance, of knowledge of one's job and, therefore, of confidence. These qualities minimize fear and maximize sound judgment under pressure and—with some of that indispensable stuff called luck—often bring success from seemingly hopeless situations."

The enemy will fight you in the area he fears you the most. To resist the temptation to wave the proverbial white flag signifying that you are giving up, take your stand in prayer. You will be equipped with the mind of Christ. Albert Einstein, in a letter to a professor emeritus of philosophy at the College of the City of New York, defending the appointment of Bertrand Russell to a teaching position stated, "Great spirits have always encountered violent opposition from mediocre minds. The mediocre mind is incapable of understanding the man who refuses to bow blindly to conventional prejudices and chooses instead to express his opinions courageously and honestly." Stand firm in your position as God's earthly representative. Be courageous. Courage will cause you to set plausible goals and dare to exceed the expectations of those who oppose you. Courage is what it takes to accomplish God's plans for your life. Courage is the womb from which great leaders, innovators, and trailblazers are birthed. Courage causes great achievers and champions to look within themselves to find the mental, moral, emotional, and spiritual strength to realize their goals, reach their fullest potential, alter their destiny, and prevail over hardship, pain, disappointment, failure, moral challenges, and mortal danger to their personal self and well-being. All of us face something that challenges us. All of us face some kind of fear. It could be fear of people, fear of ridicule, fear of being alone, fear of rejection, fear of failure, fear of change, or fear of commitment.

Did you know that everyone is challenged at some point in their life's journey with some kind of fear? Even people whom we may perceive as not having any fear at all have had moments when they had to push past fear. The blessing does not lie in having no fear, because there is healthy fear—like the fear of God. The blessing, however, lies in the efforts you make in working toward becoming mentally, emotionally, and spiritually stronger and more skillful at what you are wired to do until you are empowered to face and conquer your fears. Eleanor Roosevelt said, "The danger lies in refusing to face the fear, in not daring to come to grips with it…you must make yourself succeed every time. You must do the thing you think you cannot do."

God gave Joshua the encouragement he needed, and he went on to become one of the most powerful commanders the nation of Israel ever had. He had to learn the art of conditioning his mind to succeed at life and to win. You must learn the art of mental conditioning: "Gird up the loins of your mind" (1 Pet. 1:13). Do not quit and give into your fears. Assume the posture of a conqueror.

Hear the Word of the Lord taken from Isaiah 41:10: "Fear not, for I am with you; be not dismayed, for I am your God. I will strengthen you, yes, I will help you, I will uphold you with My righteous right hand."

If you are going to walk away from an abusive relationship, you need courage. If you are going to start a new business, you need courage. If you have to stand up for yourself and face your giant, it will take courage. It will take courage to:

+ Speak up against injustices

+ To start a new life for you and your family

+ To move from the familiar into the unfamiliar

+ To relocate

+ To resist peer pressure

+ To walk away from opportunities that offer great rewards but compromise your convictions

+ To obey God at the expense of your job, reputation, or love

- To say no when a yes is required

- To say yes to a leadership position that you think you are not qualified for

- To speak up for yourself

- To resist the temptation to retreat or stop because of opposition, criticism, or lack of support

- To start a business in spite of the lack of resources

- To go out on a limb for something you believe in

- To maintain your integrity when no one is looking

- To be yourself when it is more convenient to fit in with the crowd

- To live for God in an anti-God, anti-Christ, or anti-Semitism environment

- To maintain your purity when all your peers think you're a square

- To insist on zero defects and excellence when mediocrity is the standard

- To become a trailblazer and break the status quo

- To not allow your nationality, ethnicity, or gender prevent you from breaking glass ceilings

- To accomplish what people say can never be done

- To act as a catalyst of change within your organization, government, or community

- To bridge the gap

- To fire nonproductive employees

- To set new and clear boundaries

- To confront your abuser and say, "No more!"

- To go for what you want in spite of giants

- To swallow hard and say, "I'm sorry," "I made a mistake," "I'm guilty," "You're right and I'm wrong," "Forgive me," or "I said it, and I'm sorry."

- To go back to school after forty

+ To prove your critics wrong

+ To move on

+ To change

+ To write

+ To love again

+ To trust again

+ To believe again

+ To hope again

Courage, boldness, and confidence give us a solid footing in prayer to defeat the enemy. We have to know who we are in the spirit to move heaven; otherwise we are too timid to make a difference. In speaking of spiritual warfare, Paul tells us:

> Be strong in the Lord and in the power of His might.... Take up the whole armor of God, that you may be able to withstand in the evil day, and having done all, to *stand*.
> *Stand* therefore.
> —EPHESIANS 6:10, 13–14,
> EMPHASIS ADDED

It is time to take our positions in the field.

When Jesus was on the earth, He told His disciples:

> Behold, I give you the authority to trample on
> serpents and scorpions, and over the power of
> the enemy, and nothing shall by any means
> hurt you.
> —LUKE 10:19

One of the things we need to realize is that *authority* and *power* are different things, though we often use them interchangeably. The power is in the government or kingdom that backs the individual; authority is invested in the individual as a representative of the government or kingdom. When kingdoms clash, the military with the superior training and equipment, the one with the most sophisticated arsenal and weaponry, will be the one to emerge as the ruling power.

Our kingdom—the kingdom of heaven—has not only the power but also the authority to rule. A police officer, for example, does not have the power to stop a speeding truck like, say, Superman would, but he does have the authority invested in him by the government that issued the truck driver his license. So when a traffic officer holds up his hand at an intersection, the trucks and cars stop until the officer waves them on again. There is no magic in the officer holding up his hand to stop the traffic, but the power of his government behind him, which will inflict fines and penalties on those who don't stop when the officer motions for them to do so, gives him authority. And with this authority, his natural physical power is inconsequential. This is why the Bible instructs us in Joel 3:10, "Beat your plowshares into swords and your pruning hooks into spears; let the weak say, 'I am strong.'"

However, if the officer is operating outside of the authority vested in him, then the government will remove him and not penalize those who don't obey. Therefore we must understand the jurisdiction of our authority to exercise it correctly. Learning to pray aright is not so we can learn to speak the right words and get everything we want. The power of prayer is not merely in the words we speak but in our relationship to the One giving authority.

Thus prayer is first and foremost an essential way of opening communications with the throne room of God. You have probably heard that before, but I am hoping you will see it in a fuller light. Prayer is not a soliloquy, but a dialogue. If it is not a two-way communication, it is not prayer—not that God doesn't hear, but if we are not open and patient enough to receive the answers and strategies He sends back to us, than what is the point of inquiring of God in the first place?

Prayer is not delegation. We don't give God a "to do" list and then sit back and wait for Him to take care of things. Prayer is a partnership. There are some things—such as cares, anxieties, and hurts—that we are to bring to the feet of Jesus and leave there for Him to handle, but there are also issues we bring to Jesus for Him to pour light into so we know what to do or say. We fast and pray that we might better pierce the veil between the spiritual and physical realms—that we would be stronger in the fruit and gifts of the Spirit so we are enabled to meet the needs of others when they come to us. We make ourselves the bridge of God's love and power to the earth. We dig into prayer not that we would change God, but that He would change us.

Wherever you are in the world right now—whatever "realms" you touch as you go through each week at church, at work, in the community, as a citizen of a nation and the world—God has missions and assignments He wants taken care of. Chances are, whatever touches your heart in what you see day to day also touches the heart of God. He wants to reach out into that place and fix things, but He needs hands to reach out—and that is the responsibility of His body. He is not just asking for a hand to reach out on His behalf and do *something*; He wants it to reach out and do *His thing*. But if the hand is not in communication with the head, that failure of communication is the disconnect that keeps heaven from touching the earth.

What kind of employees think they can skip out on regular meetings with their boss and still do a good job at work? Thus the business of heaven only succeeds if its members are in regular communication with the Boss and know the Policy Manual—the Bible—by heart. There is no argument that the primary way God speaks to us is through His Word and that He never acts outside of the practices and policies He has established in the Scriptures. Thus meditating on the Scriptures is the check-and-balance system of our actions. We are people of the Spirit *and* the Word. It's not so much that they hold equal authority—it is more that they synergize one another. A person who understands her or his authority as outlined in the Word and confirmed by the Holy Spirit becomes more than the sum of the individual parts. It is much like the difference between the power of addition and the power of multiplication. The initial increments are not much different, but the further along you get, the curve starts skyrocketing almost straight up instead of each step along the way being the same increment as the step before.

Through New Eyes

Another major part of this transformational process is to begin to see things and people as God sees them. We have to give God our spiritual eyes and thoughts so that He can replace them with His.

Take, for example, Elisha's servant in 2 Kings 6:8–23. One day he arises to wander to the city gates, and before him is the host of Syria. The array of forces had been sent to kill Elisha because he had been passing intelligence about the movements of the Syrian armies to the king of Israel. Elisha's servant saw cavalry, charioteers, and foot soldiers that were more than he could count. They were in every direction, already settled in for a long siege on the city.

Scared half to death, he ran back to Elisha, woke him, and exclaimed, "Alas, my master! What shall we do?" (v. 15).

Elisha must have arisen, put on his robe, and looked out the window. I can just imagine him turning back to his servant, smiling, and saying, "Do not fear, for those who are with us are more than those who are with them" (v. 16).

I can also imagine the servant's face at that remark expressing a look that was somewhere between "Can you not count?" and "Are you completely out of your mind?" It didn't faze Elisha, though. Rather than trying to explain it to his servant, he simply bowed his head and said, "LORD, I pray, open his eyes so that he may see" (v. 17).

Instantly the multitude that had driven fear into the servant's heart was dwarfed by the multitude surrounding them. The Syrian army circled the entire city in a band of tents and fires through which no one could penetrate without being captured. Some watched the city walls with spears in their hands and horns at their sides ready to call the alert if anyone tried to leave the city. Others were cooking or eating breakfast, sharpening their weapons, or laughing with their fellow soldiers, confident that nothing in the world threatened them because of their numbers and strength.

But God opened the eyes Elisha's servant to see beyond them! Every mountain that surrounded the valley was filled with angels on horseback and in chariots of fire poised to attack! The horses pawed at the ground, barely able to constrain themselves from galloping upon the enemies of the people of God to trample them into the dust, mist shooting from their nostrils in the cold morning air. Suddenly the fear of the Syrians evaporated at the sight of the host beyond them! When you learn to fear the things of God, what on the surface of the earth can ever make you fear again?

We must learn to see with our spiritual eyes as readily as we see with our physical eyes. We must come to the understanding of how much greater God is than anything we could face here on the earth. We have to dig into the spirit in prayer so that we are comfortable with God's realm and how it functions. And, of course, the Bible is our handbook for all things spiritual. It is spiritual food that strengthens and nurtures the human spirit within us. It is the personal trainer of the soul so that we can discern the thoughts and intents of the heart. (See Hebrews 4:12.)

Because the battles that we fight are mental battles, we must realize that our losses don't come because we don't have the Word of God. We do have it, but we don't embrace all that it promises to us. It is one thing to understand the promise, but another to allow the Word of God to fortify your mind so you have more confidence in the spiritual realm than you do in the physical. Too often we get overwhelmed because of what we see in the natural realm as opposed to the forces of God that are backing us up. The things of the spirit are eternal and unbeatable. We must learn how to delve into the unseen realm; it has resources we will never have access to in the natural, physical world.

To this end we have what you might call some "double-whammy" passages in the Bible that are provided for us by the apostle Paul. They are like the one-two punch or rope-a-dope blows of boxing, because they are God-dictated scriptural prayers combining the Word and the Spirit into one. I believe the most refined of these are found in the Book of Ephesians, which in a lot of ways is Paul's final thesis on the composition, function, and purpose of the church. It was one of his last letters and therefore expresses a lifetime of seeking God to understand the age he lived in—what is known as the church age. It is so significant that even in the midst of writing it Paul can't help but break out into prayer.

In this book Paul offers two prayers. The first is found in chapter 1:

> Therefore I also, after I heard of your faith in the Lord Jesus and your love for all the saints, do not cease to give thanks for you, making mention of you in my prayers: that the God of our Lord Jesus Christ, the Father of glory, may give to you the spirit of wisdom and

revelation in the knowledge of Him, the eyes of your understanding being enlightened; that you may know what is the hope of His calling, what are the riches of the glory of His inheritance in the saints, and what is the exceeding greatness of His power toward us who believe, according to the working of His mighty power which He worked in Christ when He raised Him from the dead and seated Him at His right hand in the heavenly places, far above all principality and power and might and dominion, and every name that is named, not only in this age but also in that which is to come. And He put all things under His feet, and gave Him to be head over all things to the church, which is His body, the fullness of Him who fills all in all.

—EPHESIANS 1:15–23

The second is from chapter 3:

For this reason I bow my knees to the Father of our Lord Jesus Christ, from whom the whole family in heaven and earth is named, that He would grant you, according to the riches of His glory, to be strengthened with might through His Spirit in the inner man, that Christ may dwell in your hearts through faith; that you, being rooted and grounded in love, may be able to comprehend with all the saints what is the width and length and depth and height—to know the love of Christ which passes knowledge; that you may be filled with all the fullness of God. Now to Him who is able to do exceedingly abundantly above all that we ask or think, according to the power that works in us, to Him be glory in the church by Christ Jesus to all generations, forever and ever. Amen.

—Ephesians 3:14–21

In these prayers Paul asks God for basically eight different things that every born-again believer needs and has a right to. They are the foundation of understanding who we became when we changed citizenship from the kingdom of this earth to the kingdom of heaven, and they are what every person on the earth needs in order to know who God truly is. In the order he prays them, they are:

1. That you would fully receive the Holy Spirit—the Spirit of wisdom and revelation—that He would daily increase your knowledge of God.

2. That your eyes—both physical and spiritual—would be flooded with light and opened to God's truths and that you would understand the ultimate goal—the hope—of the calling God has on your life.

3. That you might understand the riches and resources of what it means to be called by God and what you have a right to inherit as a coheir with Jesus.

4. That you would understand the limitlessness of His power, the very power He used to raise Jesus from the dead and wants to use on your behalf as well.

5. That God the Father would strengthen you from the inside out through His Holy Spirit.

6. That the same Christ anointing that was upon Jesus would dwell within you through your faith.

7. That you would be grounded with roots that sink down deeply in the love of God, giving you an

understanding and knowledge of all
of its dimensions, an understanding
that is only possible as you join and
work elbow to elbow corporately with
other believers.

8. That you would be filled with all that
God is—His power, His righteousness, His glory, His all! Because, after
all, He is and can do far more than
you can imagine or dream to ask!

I'm telling you, these scriptural prayers and points
are worth some major meditation time! In fact, great
ministers have spent weeks and months praying these
prayers over and over for themselves or those they
wanted to see come to a saving knowledge of Jesus
Christ. I believe that as you pray these scriptures and
meditate on the verses of Ephesians, God will reveal
to you the true standing of grace and authority you
have before Him, a place to stand in the courtroom
of heaven with Jesus beside you as your Advocate,
presenting your case and that of others before the
judgment seat of the Father. The confidence, faith,
and boldness with which you take your stand in
prayer are critical to the presentation of your appeals

and requests. Your communication in the Spirit with your Advocate, Jesus Christ, gives you revolutionary insight into how to correctly present your case and "reason together" (Isa. 1:18) with God so you receive the answers and strategies you need.

We must come into a full understanding of who we become when we cross the border from the kingdom of this world into the kingdom of God. There is so much in us that comes through the love of God shed abroad in our hearts and the new standing we have before the Father because of what Jesus accomplished on the cross and from the tomb. To that end I have also included an appendix that has a list of scriptures that tell us who we instantly become when we choose to be "in Christ." I urge you to take that list and mediate upon it, ruminate over those scriptures, and let them build a foundation within you so you might begin to see yourself as God sees you. For who you truly are is only who God says that you are—no other opinion, failure, accomplishment, or judgment matters. It is in realizing who God says that we are that we gain the confidence, faith, and boldness to argue effectively before the court of heaven to pull down its blessings, wisdom, and resource into the earth.

We have some work to do in the spirit. This kind of change doesn't happen overnight, but it happens gradually and progressively as we seek to understand the realm of the spiritual better than we understand the world we physically walk in every day. As we do, the transformation that is possible is beyond anything that has yet been imagined. We must not be limited by the thinking of the world around us. God has more, and He is anxious to release it into the earth, but He can only do it through His body. If it is going to happen, then it is going to come through us, and it is only going to come through us if we understand how to pray and hear from heaven in revolutionary new ways.

Three

SYNCING HEART
and PRACTICE

Understanding the Tactics of Prayer

Strategy is a system of expedients [options]. It is more
than science; it is the translation of science into prac-
tical life, the development of an original leading thought
in accordance with the ever-changing circumstances.
—HELMUTH VON MOLTKE

ALL OF HER life she had been consumed by
one thing. She wanted a son. It burned
a hole in her heart. It upset her husband.
It upset her family. It would have been better for
everyone if she would have just left it alone and let
it go, but she couldn't. No one understood it, and
as a result no one seemed to understand her. Even
her priest didn't understand it but thought the passion with which she prayed was the result of being

inebriated. But she knew differently. Spiritually she was pregnant with a prophet of God, but she had to birth him first in prayer before she could birth him in the natural. It is funny how many really important things come that way.

But if she hadn't stuck with it in prayer, what would have happened to Samuel? Would he have ever been born? Would David have ever been king? How different might the history of the nation of Israel been—let alone the entire world—had Hannah not battled for her child in the spirit. It is mind-boggling but true—when Hannah was pregnant with a son, heaven was pregnant with a prophet and two kings. God gave her the desire of her heart, because it was the desire of God's heart. All she needed to do was pray through until heaven broke through the resistance. She literally prayed heaven down.

Many believers are desperate for a breakthrough. But breakthroughs have to be pursued. You must prevail over territorial spirits in order to possess your possessions. You must activate and exercise your dominion over a region within a realm, system, kingdom, industry, field, and discipline. In 2 Samuel 23:13–16 we read of David's quest to quench his thirst. He had a divine desire for that which God had prepared for him before the foundation of the world.

Then three of the thirty chief men went down at harvest time and came to David at the cave of Adullam. And the troop of Philistines encamped in the Valley of Rephaim. David was then in the stronghold, and the garrison of the Philistines was then in Bethlehem. And David said with longing, "Oh, that someone would give me a drink of the water from the well of Bethlehem, which is by the gate!" So the three mighty men broke through the camp of the Philistines, drew water from the well of Bethlehem that was by the gate, and took it and brought it to David.

In this text the enemies of David had set up a barricade to prevent him from getting what really belonged to him. His military generals broke through the barricade in order to confiscate that which belonged to David from the hands of the enemy. The enemy had assumed squatter's rights until David enforced his legal authority over a region that belonged to him. The enemy seized his property and wealth. Likewise the enemy has illegally seized many of our possessions and must be made to give them back—our reputation, our marriages, our children, our communities, our nations. He will not give them up until we demand it. We must learn how to pound at the gates of heaven through prayer and demand restitution for what he has stolen. He is a thief and must release what rightfully belongs to each of us.

A lot of people look for a rulebook for prayer. They want step one, two, three, and so on, so that they don't have to think or really pour that much of themselves into their prayers. They want to just check off the steps and feel that they have done their duty. But prayer doesn't work like that. Battles don't work like that. While you may have a plan going into the fight, once you have made first contact with the enemy, everything changes. Will you stay the course even if other people call you crazy? Will you let yourself get so deeply into prayer, let so much of yourself be invested in prayer, that you feel like you may die if you don't get what you are praying for? Desperate times call for desperate prayers. I am not saying that it will necessarily be that way, but it was for Hannah. She was so obsessed with birthing what heaven had put in her heart that nothing else mattered. And if one way failed, she quickly moved to another, because she knew it wasn't about following the right steps or behaving in a particular manner. It was about sincerely connecting with heaven, to bring forth what heaven had seeded in her heart and bring into the earth something that would change the course of nations.

Prayer, like fighting on a battlefield, is often more about adaptation than it is about the soundness of the plan we take into it. It is about cooperating and less about coercing. Will we allow God to change us once we get into the midst of the fight? It can mean the difference between success and failure. When you pray, you are often engaging the enemy of doubt, frustration, antagonism, and the disbelief hidden in the heart of others. They may not see what you are seeing— those things that God shows you by revelation or places in your heart as a desire. Once you engage the enemy, if you zig where your original battle plan said to zig, you may be in for defeat. A good general, as the German General Helmuth von Moltke advocated, has to look at all of his options for each decision, not just act according to preconceived notions. In the heat of battle the wise general will read the field and adapt his original battle plan to match what he is seeing— he has to be open to zagging when his original plan said he should be zigging. The zig-zag is our metaphor for remaining flexible. You have to cooperate with the choreographic movement of the Spirit. In the heat of the battle you must learn how to discern the flow by listening to heaven's intelligence reports so that you can understand the players involved, the spiritual terrain you must travel, as well as a myriad of other things. The general who wins is not always the one with the most apparent sophisticated battle plan going in but the one who adapts the best and responds effectively as the battle is taking place.

Prayer is no different. In fact, the most critical thing in prayer is probably how we respond to the intelligence of heaven as we receive it. In reading the writings of the great prayer warriors of the past and talking to those who have given themselves to prayer and intercession today, there is no handbook or set of rules that governs prayer in any absolute way. In speaking with a student at the International House of Prayer in Kansas City, the question on the table was geared toward ascertaining if there were special classes on prayer they were required to take. He answered, "No, but we are required to spend twenty-four hours a week in the prayer room." The pragmatism of prayer is that it is learned in the practice, not in principle. It is a journey that is first individual—"When you pray, go into your room, and when you have shut the door, pray to your Father who is in the secret place" (Matt. 6:6)—and then cooperate—"These all continued with one accord in prayer and supplication…altogether the number of names was about a hundred and twenty" (Acts 1:14–15).

I believe prayer is one of the most powerful

contributions a Christian can give toward making this world a better place. You don't learn to pray powerfully and effectively by reading a how-to manual. You learn to pray when you pray. When you do, you will discover that there is no continent, no nation, no organization, no city, no office, no situation, no circumstance, no condition, no government, no case, no issue, no battle that is off limits to the force of its effect. There is no person, no policy, nor any political power on this earth that can keep prayer out. Prayer is a game changer. Prayer makes a difference. Without prayer our Christian life is just trying to follow a list of dos and don'ts given to us by someone else. With prayer Christianity is vital, relevant, transformational, and filled with the knowledge and presence of God. If prayer was a sport, then it would be a contact sport. Prayer is the contact point between heaven and earth— or perhaps it is better said that the person who prays is that contact point. Your place of prayer is your place of power. Your place of prayer is your place of change management. We can create change through force of will and clever persuasion, but it won't last. Real, irrevocable change only comes through prayer.

So what I would like to do in this chapter is not give you rules for prayer but a list of different prayer strategies—expedients as General von Moltke would have called them—that will act as guidelines to your prayers. It is like having a toolbox of different tactics alongside you as you go into prayer and ask the Holy Spirit to guide you in how to pray effectively for whatever supplication or intercession you are bringing to God. They are like the pirate's code in *Pirates of the Caribbean*: "They aren't really rules; they're more like guidelines."

With that in mind, I would like to give you sixty different tactics to consider as you pray, but, once again, I don't have room to give them all to you in these pages. So I will give you a taste of them here by highlighting the first ten and then urge you to get my MP3 message called "The Unconventional Weapon: Sixty Ways to Pray."*

In this message I teach about all sixty of the different tactics of the unconventional weapon of prayer that God has revealed to me as I have prayed. I hope having these milling around in the back of your mind for the Holy Spirit to bring to your remembrance will at some point give you the key you need for whatever you are praying for.

---

* Available at www.trimminternational.org

TEN TACTICS OF PRAYER

1. Pray faithfully.

When you pray, ensure that you do not waver in your faith. Hold fast to what you have learned and the confidence you have received in your relationship with Christ. God can resurrect a dead life, a dead dream—anything that is dead, if you have faith: "God…gives life to the dead and calls those things which do not exist as though they did" (Rom. 4:17). If God can quicken the dead, He can bring your marriage, your business, your job, and your faith back into divine alignment with His promises. But most of the time this takes more than sending up a quick "Help me, God!" It takes dedicated, faithful, faith-filled prayer in which you present yourself to God ready to change and ready to do what He asks of you.

2. Pray decisively.

You cannot be wishy-washy when you pray—one day you trust God, the next day you don't. One day you pray this, the next day you want the opposite. You say one thing to God in faith, and then you go have coffee with your friends and talk about how it can never happen. You are wishy-washy with what you want and where you are going. As the Bible says:

> Let us hold fast the confession of our hope without wavering, for He who promised is faithful.
>
> —HEBREWS 10:23

And:

> If any of you lacks wisdom, let him ask of God, who gives to all liberally and without reproach, and it will be given to him. But let him ask in faith, with no doubting, for he who doubts is like a wave of the sea driven and tossed by the wind. For let not that man suppose that he will receive anything from the Lord; he is a double-minded man, unstable in all his ways.
>
> —JAMES 1:5–8

Let there be no misunderstanding: you can speak words in prayer that you do not believe, and they will not produce any result. Parroting something you have heard someone else say or read somewhere without conviction does not produce divine alignment. Make a deliberate and conscious decision to agree with the Word of God, and then set your heart to believe it and your mouth to speak it no matter what.

3. Pray forcefully.

Don't be a wimp! Matthew 11:12 tells us that, "The kingdom of heaven suffers violence, and the violent take it by force." You are not begging, you are not crying, and you are not persuading; you are coming to take what is legally yours according to the Word of God. You must come boldly as a child would to a father, as a prince or princess would to a king, as a wronged plaintiff would to a court of law.

Hebrews 11:6 tells us, "Without faith it is impossible to please Him, for he who comes to God must believe that He is, and that He is a rewarder of those who diligently seek Him." If you feel like you have to beg God for what He has promised, then you don't know the God of heaven. He is a rewarder. He isn't stingy in fulfilling His Word. But if you don't walk into His presence like you belong there, then your faith and understanding need an upgrade. It is not that you aren't humble; it's that you know God for the loving Father He really is.

4. Pray lovingly.

We are not called to take vengeance on anyone or any group of people—if vengeance is to be taken, it will be God taking it, not us. We are not called to be judges over the perpetrators of any crimes, disasters, or diseases. We are called to be deliverers, rescuers, and healers. We are called, like Moses when he lifted up the bronze serpent (Num. 21:4–8), to put ourselves between the people and the harm, lifting up Jesus so that those who will look up from this world to Him might also be saved. (See John 3:14–15.)

Because of this we must pray to see those who hurt us or the people we are praying for through the eyes of God. We must pray that God stops them in their tracks as He did Paul and turns them around. We cannot have faith for something if we are not walking in love, for the only thing that avails is "faith working through love" (Gal. 5:6).

5. Pray truthfully.

There are times when we are honestly in denial about the truth of a situation, or we could just be mistaken about the facts or in how we are interpreting things. But one of the names of the Holy Spirit is "the Spirit of Truth." If we will open ourselves to Him in prayer and listen more than we speak, then there is room for the Holy Spirit to adjust our perspective. He will give us the perspective from the throne room of God that we would never get on our own.

Also, we don't necessarily need to be praying "the facts"; we need to be praying the truth. The facts might be that the doctor said you will die in six months, but the truth is "by His stripes we are healed" (Isa. 53:5). The facts might be your husband is not acting lovingly toward you, but the truth is "the unbelieving husband is sanctified by the wife" (1 Cor. 7:14) and "for how do you know, O wife, whether you will save your husband?" (v. 16). The facts may be that you have a lot of unpaid bills sitting on your desk, but the truth is, "My God shall supply all your need according to His riches in glory by Christ Jesus" (Phil. 4:19). God doesn't need us to tell Him the facts—He knows them better than we do—but He does need us to agree with His promises so that we can receive the provision He desires to provide. After all, the Bible doesn't say, "You shall recognize the facts and the facts will set you free," but it says, "You shall know the truth, and the truth shall make you free" (John 8:32).

6. Pray steadfastly.

Prayer is never wasted. The Bible tells us to "be steadfast, immovable, always abounding in the work of the Lord, knowing that your labor is not in vain in the Lord" (1 Cor. 15:58). I know from personal experience that one minute in prayer can accomplish more than a lifetime of other activities. Hold fast to God's promises in prayer no matter what things look like in the natural—God will answer you if you seek Him with all of your heart. (See Jeremiah 29:11–14.)

7. Pray earnestly.

Life throws us curveballs, and though we have different backgrounds and personal histories, we all have emotions, dreams, and passions. When we are emotionally involved in a struggle, we tend to pray less rather than pray more. If we are to have overcoming prayer lives, we need to turn those emotions and passions into prayer rather than let them become a hindrance to it. We are told:

> Elijah was a man with a nature like ours, and he prayed earnestly that it would not rain; and it did not rain on the land for three years and six months. And he prayed again, and the heaven gave rain, and the earth produced its fruit.
>
> —JAMES 5:17–18

The King James Version of this says Elijah "was a man subject to like passions as we are," but that when he prayed earnestly, God still heard Him. He knew how to engage the God that answers by fire. Jacob had to wrestle with God to get His blessing. (See Genesis 32:22–32.) We have to come to God earnestly as who we are and be willing to stay in prayer—even if we are angry or frustrated—until we get God's answer. God understands emotions—He created them! We have to be willing to express them earnestly as much as we need to be ready for God to change or correct them.

8. Pray positionally.

As we discussed in the last chapter, we have to know where we stand in order to pray effectively. We know we are seated in heavenly places in Christ Jesus (look at Appendix B to better understand what it means to be "in Christ") and that Jesus "always lives to make intercession" (Heb. 7:25). Thus the best place for us to be praying is from our position "in Christ," praying the same intercessions He is praying over every situation. As we discussed in *The Art of War for Spiritual Battle*, this was the breakthrough that came to John "Praying" Hyde, who said, "So I confess my ever-failing prayers...and plead His never failing intercession."[1] We must pray "in Christ" as the very person the "in Christ" scriptures tell us we are.

9. Pray authoritatively.

Praying in Jesus' name is not just a closing we are supposed to use before we say, "Amen." Praying in the name of Jesus is coming to the throne of God just as an ambassador would come to the throne of a foreign king "in the name of" his own king. Using the name of Jesus is another "in Christ" privilege and signet of our authority as a representative of Jesus. As Scripture says:

> And whatever you ask in My name, that I will do, that the Father may be glorified in the Son. If you ask anything in My name, I will do it.
> —JOHN 14:13–14

And:

> Therefore God also has highly exalted Him and given Him the name which is above every name, that at the name of Jesus every knee should bow, of those in heaven, and of those on earth, and of those under the earth, and that every tongue should confess that Jesus Christ is Lord, to the glory of God the Father.
> —PHILIPPIANS 2:9–11

When we pray in the name of Jesus, we pray in the authority of Jesus. The name of Jesus will give you the power to overcome when you truly pray in that name.

10. Pray masterfully.

To gain mastery in a thing, you must practice it continually. Malcolm Gladwell talks about the "10,000-Hour Rule" in his best-selling book *Outliers*. The principle is that those who are most successful at a thing are those who have spent the most time, at the right time, doing that thing. Charles Spurgeon said it this way, "Pray until you can really pray."

As I have already said, prayer is a journey that is unique for each one of us. Just as each of us has a different calling or job to do for God, each of us will travel a slightly different road in understanding what prayer really is. God will speak to each of us in different ways, and the way God speaks to one person can be markedly different from the way He speaks to another. Why? Because God isn't interested in getting us to learn rules and requirements and living life merely by following the dictates of a rulebook, but He wants us to come to Him that we might know Him for ourselves. He wants a unique relationship with each of us just as He created each of us as unique individuals. He wants to partner with us in our journey and live it out with us day by day. It is why He created human beings in the first place, and it is His great joy when we come to Him without doubt or compromise to wholeheartedly get to know Him and let ourselves be fully known by Him. God is all about relationship, and the key to it is masterful prayer.

THE BEAUTY OF BEING UNCONVENTIONAL

There is an often-quoted saying that "if you do what you have always done, you will get what you have always gotten." In other words, if you want to grow, if you want to progress, if you want to experience something new, then you have to do things differently than you have ever done them before.

To a certain extent, learning to pray is a trial-and-error experience. On many levels it is as simple as opening our hearts to heaven and telling God how we feel—something so simple children are naturals at it—but it is also sublime. A lifetime spent in prayer will never be monotonous unless we pull back and stop growing in its practice. It is a unique journey God has designed for each of us. That is not to say that we can't learn about prayer from one another—otherwise what would be the point of writing all of these books on it? But it does mean that if all you do is read these books, you will never really understand what prayer is all about. I can tell you, but you have to experience it for yourself to understand it.

However, when you pray only in isolation and without learning about what prayer has done through others, you can miss the possibilities of prayer, or grow discouraged, because seeking God in prayer—to the point you really and consistently hear from heaven—is not an undertaking for the faint of heart! You have to stick with it. You have to read about it and learn how prayer has touched the lives of others. Surround yourself with people who pray. Let them inspire you to get back into your closet and pray where only God can see and hear you. You have to be there when your church calls prayer meetings and inspire confidence in prayer in other believers. You can never, never, never let prayer become a stagnant part of your life. It is vital to who you are as a Christian and even more vital to fulfilling God's mission and your assignment upon the earth.

There is nothing more pleasing to the devil than a Christian who doesn't pray, because that person is someone he doesn't have to waste his time worrying about. In fact, his overall strategy over the years seems to be to get us too busy to pray and for us to think that we don't really need to pray because God already knows our needs, so why bother Him with them by praying? However, John Wesley famously said, "I pray two hours every morning. That is if I don't have a lot to do. If I have a lot to do for that day, then I pray three hours."

I want to see your prayer life reinvigorated. I want you to have breakthroughs in prayer that will astound you. I am praying that is exactly what happens for everyone who reads my books on the subject. There is so much to do, it can't be done without each of us playing our parts, and our parts won't be done if we don't learn what they are in prayer. As you will see more clearly in the next chapter, time is of the essence.

Four

"*For* SUCH *a* TIME *as* THIS"

Understanding Prophecy's Bearing on Prayer

For the testimony [lifestyle] of Jesus is the spirit of prophecy.
—REVELATION 19:10

THE PRESIDENT GLANCED furtively about the room. No one returned his gaze, but he couldn't get over the feeling he was being watched, even here in the council chambers of the government. As he rose to leave, he could feel the eyes on him from every direction—questioning eyes, wondering eyes, but most of all eyes that seemed filled with envy and condemnation every time he spoke. As one of the sole administrators remaining from the conquered Babylonian Empire, he had expected jealousies—and the fact that he was Jewish didn't help much either—but things were worse than even that. The counsel chambers, filled with ambitious, young bureaucrats and military officers vying for King Darius's favor, filled with murmuring and disapproving glances every time the king asked for Daniel's advice. They were seldom pleased with his plans that they saw as too cautious, too self-righteous, and filled with too much pandering for the populace at large. They were conquerors, after all, not nursemaids or prayer warriors. What did they care if some poor slob of a peasant got injured building the new palace because "proper precautions" weren't taken? They wanted to get things done, and they didn't mind cutting corners to do it. Despite the fact that Daniel was from the occupied government, Darius seemed to trust Daniel's advice more with each passing day. If fact, the king seemed to actually prefer Daniel's counsel to that of his own generals because he didn't cut corners. His credibility and widespread influence grew out of his integrity. This wasn't winning him many friends. (I don't want you to miss this point, so I will say it more plainly. When kingdoms clash, your credibility and influence grow in proportion to your integrity. You must be committed to the cause, even when falsely accused. Very often, as God increases your influence, your competitors will come for your jugular—your integrity.)

As Daniel headed for the door, there was

something else that seemed much more important pricking at his mind than court politics. For days and weeks something kept tugging at the back of his mind, rumbling around inside of him like a premonition he couldn't quite put into words. Something wasn't right, and it had far greater import than the rumors he had heard about the plots against his life. He was so consumed by his thoughts that he didn't even notice when groups of people fell silent at the sight of him as he made his way through the halls of government toward his home. His personal bodyguard had to almost jog to keep up with his pace. Despite being over ninety years old, Daniel was still incredibly spry.

As he made his way through the city market, a thought was forming in the back of his mind that he had to double-check—something he had read some time ago, something the prophet Jeremiah had recorded—what exactly had he said again? It was a prophecy he had given the year Daniel was taken as a teenager to live in Nebuchadnezzar's palace, something about when all of this was supposed to change.

Entering his home, he waved away offers of food from his servants without even looking at them, threw his official robe of state to one of his footmen, and headed for the library. "I am not to be disturbed," he informed them as he shut the doors behind him.

The lamplight flickered against the growing dusk as Daniel scanned the shelves of scrolls. Finding a newly recopied parchment of the prophecies of Jeremiah, Daniel took it carefully from the self, sat at one of the tables, and began reading. After nearly an hour he found what he was after: a passage that spoke of when the Jews would be allowed to return to their homeland and rebuild Jerusalem:

> And this whole land shall be a desolation and an astonishment, and these nations shall serve the king of Babylon seventy years. "Then it will come to pass, when seventy years are completed, that I will punish the king of Babylon and that nation, the land of the Chaldeans, for their iniquity," says the LORD.
> —JEREMIAH 25:11–12

Referring to his journals, his collection of histories, and his calendars, he recalculated the number of years since Jerusalem had been laid waste—a figure he knew by heart but wanted to cross-check with as many sources as he could—and Judah had been carried off as slaves into Babylon. Just as he already knew, the seventy years were nearing their end.

Daniel remembered the vision God had shown

him almost five decades back—just a few years after he had been brought to Nebuchadnezzar's palace. The king had had a dream he couldn't remember, and he was livid that none of his "wise" men could give him the interpretation of it. Daniel prayed, and God showed it to him. It was a statue with a head of gold, chest and arms of silver, torso of bronze, legs of iron, and feet of iron and clay mixed together. God revealed to Daniel that the gold head represented the Babylonian Empire and the others the empires to follow. Every preceding kingdom would be conquered by another kingdom seemingly inferior in substance than the first. What kingdom would it be that characterized the "stone kingdom"? And how could a kingdom of stone emerge as the most powerful of all? This kingdom was depicted as the foot in Nebuchadnezzar's dream. (God has given us authority and dominion through Jesus Christ to tread on the enemy. We must put our foot down.)

Years later Daniel had another vision that seemed to repeat the one of the statue. This time it was of four beasts: a lion with eagle's wings that rose to turn into a man, the second was like a bear, the third like a leopard with four bird wings, and the fourth a beast with ten horns. He was told these represented four kings of the future, but he was unsure of what to make of them or if they had any relationship to the kingdoms of the statue.

Then, a short time later, Daniel was given another vision, one of a ram and a goat, again representing two kingdoms to come. The angel Gabriel told him they were the Medo-Persian and then the Greek empires. The experience had left him weak, and he was bedridden for some time. It had also left him more puzzled than ever before about what God was trying to tell him.

Then Daniel thought over the last year or so of his life. Just months ago the last Babylonian emperor, Belshazzar, had roused him from his bed to come interpret a sign he was seeing. Daniel was sure that Belshazzar had merely been drinking too much again, but all the same he fought off sleep and impatience trying to rouse himself to be pleasant, and he opened his heart to hear what God would have him say to his ruler. That night a disembodied hand wrote on the wall of the emperor's chamber, and Belshazzar was "weighed in the balances, and found wanting" (Dan. 5:27). He died that very night, killed as the Medes took the palace in a swift assault. Babylon was destroyed, just as Jeremiah had foreseen that it would be in the text Daniel had just read— but then why was Judah still in captivity despite the fulfillment of what the prophet had been shown?

In that moment Daniel knew he had to act. Before him was the prophetic code deciphered. He realized he was at the turning point of one prophetic age into another. So Daniel went into action. He fell to his knees and began to pray.

UNDERSTANDING OUR PROPHETIC AGE

I am not sure how familiar you are with end-times prophecy—and I don't really have room in this book to do a thorough job of explaining it all—but let me give you the "trimmed" version. While there are various interpretations of how all of this will come about, if you look at three main texts—what I call the "three peaks"—I think it is easy to get a general outline of what we will see in the days to come. The first is Daniel 9:24–27, the second is Ezekiel 36–39, and the third is Matthew 24.

When Daniel bowed his knee that day in early Persia, God answered his prayer by revealing to him the final plan for the salvation of His people as well as all those who would call on the name of His Son. It is such a key passage that it has been called "the continental divide of Bible prophecy." Everything before it had been about the Law of Moses and showing its inability to completely save; everything after it would be about God's plan to save by sending His Son as a sacrificial offering that would once and for all fulfill the law and bring salvation to all who called Jesus their Lord and Savior. Living by the Law of the Old Testament and being the nation of God on the earth had come to a crashing failure in Daniel's lifetime as both Israel and Judah were dismantled because they had failed to follow God. Yet even at the pinnacle of their failure, God revealed to them the promise of their future and ultimate redemption.

In a nutshell, in answer to his prayer an angel came to Daniel and told him of seventy weeks in which God would work His ultimate salvation plan. Commonly referred to as "Daniel's Seventy Weeks," this plan was laid out in Daniel 9:24–27 (NAS):

> Seventy weeks have been decreed for your people and your holy city, to finish the transgression, to make an end of sin, to make atonement for iniquity, to bring in everlasting righteousness, to seal up vision and prophecy and to anoint the most holy place. So you are to know and discern that from the issuing of a decree to restore and rebuild Jerusalem until Messiah the Prince

there will be seven weeks and sixty-two weeks; it will be built again, with plaza and moat, even in times of distress. Then after the sixty-two weeks the Messiah will be cut off and have nothing, and the people of the prince who is to come will destroy the city and the sanctuary. And its end will come with a flood; even to the end there will be war; desolations are determined. And he will make a firm covenant with the many for one week, but in the middle of the week he will put a stop to sacrifice and grain offering; and on the wing of abominations will come one who makes desolate, even until a complete destruction, one that is decreed, is poured out on the one who makes desolate.

That may seem a little obscure, but in it God shows Daniel three periods of time (with another imbedded in the gap between the last two) totaling seventy weeks that would happen before "everlasting righteousness" was released into the earth:

1. After the decree to rebuild Jerusalem went out, there would be seven weeks before the work was finished.

2. Then sixty-two weeks more would pass until the Messiah would be revealed and then "cut off."

3. Then the last week would begin when "the prince who is to come"—aka the Antichrist—made a peace treaty with Israel and began the Tribulation.

In this prophecy each week represents a period of 7 years, and at that time the Jewish year was measured by cycles of the moon rather than our rotation around the sun—so each year was 360 days, not 365 as we know a year today. From the time the decree to rebuild Jerusalem went out in 445 B.C. (see Nehemiah 2:6–8) until the work was finished, it would be 49 years (7 times 7 years), and from the time of the decree until the revelation of the Messiah would be 69 weeks, or 483 Jewish years.

In the late 1800s, a Scotland Yard detective by the name of Robert Anderson sat down with these numbers to do an exact calculation. He chose the Jewish month of Nissan in 445 B.C. as his starting point and then determined that 483 Jewish years would be 173,880 days. Then, switching to the Gregorian calendar as we use it today, he determined that the first of Nissan 445 B.C. would be March 14 of that year. Moving forward in time 173,880 days brought him to April 6, A.D. 32, the Sunday before Passover of that year according to historical records—or more significantly, the day we refer to as Palm Sunday, the day of Jesus' triumphant entrance into Jerusalem the weekend before He was raised from the dead. According to Scripture, this is the only day on which Jesus allowed Himself to be publicly heralded as the Messiah. With the exact date of Jesus' birth uncertain as the year 0, it is easy to see that April 6, 32 fits surprisingly accurately to the time the first Easter may have actually taken place.

This passage then states that after the Messiah is cut off, there will be a period in which the Antichrist destroys Jerusalem and the temple—which happened in 70 under the troops led by the future Roman emperor Titus—during which there would be constant war, only ending after a seven-year peace treaty is signed between the nation of Israel and the world figure who would later be revealed to be the Antichrist himself. This period of time would be the church age, the age we are presently living in, which began with the resurrection of Jesus Christ and will end when the Tribulation, or seventieth week of Daniel, begins.

But when would this period near its end? What

would be the key events to watch for before the beginning of Daniel's final week? These are given to us in two other passages—Ezekiel 36–39 and Matthew 24 by Jesus Himself.

It is important to realize that Ezekiel was alive at the same time that Daniel was, and if Bible scholars are correct in their dating, the prophecies of Ezekiel 36–39 were given the same year Nebuchadnezzar sacked Jerusalem while Daniel was a young man serving in Nebuchadnezzar's court roughly eighteen years after Daniel had interpreted the dream of the statue representing five kingdoms to the king. While Daniel was given the overarching outline of God's plan for redemption, Ezekiel was given the next prophetic event—the return of the Jews to the nation of Israel to renew self-rule.

All generations since the time of Paul have looked to the heavens hoping to see Jesus' return, but not all generations have had the signs given in Scripture line up to indicate it could happen. The first and most important of these signs was the return of the Jews to their homeland to reestablish the nation of Israel, which happened in 1948 and was foretold by Ezekiel. It is easy to underestimate the significance of this prophecy. First of all, no nation that has ever been conquered and dispersed (all Jews were exiled from

Judea by the Romans as a result of the Bar Kokhba revolt in 135) has ever returned to the same place to reestablish itself as a nation, let alone it happening after nearly two millennia with every other nation in the region opposing it. From the time of Jerusalem being sacked by Nebuchadnezzar until May 15, 1948, Israel was always either under the rule of another empire or scattered around the world. It is amazing that the Hebrew people were able to preserve themselves culturally, let alone ethnically, during that time. Even during Jesus' time Israel was not independent but was under Roman rule. In fact, it was because the Jews looked for the Messiah to deliver them politically that so many misunderstood the spiritual kingdom about which Jesus preached and taught.

When Israel again became a nation in 1948, it was as if a prophetic clock that had long been halted began counting down again. When Jesus was asked in Matthew 24:3, "What will be the sign of Your coming, and of the end of the age?", He gave eight distinct signs that would increase in frequency and intensity as the time drew nearer:

1. "Many will come in My name, saying, 'I am the Christ,' and will mislead many" (v. 5).

2. "You will hear of wars and rumors of wars" (v. 6).

3. "Nation will rise against nation, and kingdom against kingdom" (v. 7).

4. "There will be famines, pestilences, and earthquakes in various places" (v. 7).

5. "Then they will deliver you to tribulation and kill you, and you will be hated by all nations for My name's sake" (v. 9).

6. "Many will be offended, will betray one another, and will hate one another. Then many false prophets will rise up and deceive many" (vv. 10–11).

7. "Because lawlessness will abound, the love of many will grow cold" (v. 12),

8. "This gospel of the kingdom will be preached in all the world" (v. 14).

While entire books have been written discussing the increase of these signs, it doesn't take a rocket scientist to read the daily paper and see these things are increasing. There are more cults and new religions today than in the history of the world, and they are increasing at an exponential rate. All you have to do is turn on the TV to hear of rumors of wars, and some wars have been going on for so long that they don't even make the news anymore. Persecution has been greater in the last century than all the rest of history combined, and while earthquakes have only been measurable since 1900, three of the top ten have all happened in the last eight years. With the Arab Spring and its repercussions, faction continues to rise against faction—and while the gospel goes forth with great vigor in some areas, others are growing lukewarm and cold in their faith while churches become more and more focused on earthly rather than eternal success.

Yet perhaps the most important prophecy of all is found a little later in verses 32–34:

> Now learn this parable from the fig tree: When its branch has already become tender and puts forth leaves, you know that summer is near. So you also, when you see all these things, know that it is near—at the doors! Assuredly, I say to you, this generation will by no means pass away till all these things take place.

Time and again throughout Scripture the fig tree is used to represent the nations of Israel. So when Jesus talks of the fig tree putting forth leaves, He is talking about the blossoming of the reborn state of Israel as we know it today. The generation that was born the year of Israel's rebirth would be in their sixties as I write this, and the generation born when Israel expanded to its present borders are in their mid-forties. When exactly that part of the clock started, I don't know, but I have to believe whichever that generation is, it is on the earth today.

Add to this that many end-times teachers point to the time before the beginning of the Tribulation and the Rapture as likely to be the greatest time of revival that ever hits the earth. (Look at Matthew 24:14 again; also, James 5:7 says before the end, God will receive "the precious fruit of the earth.") Already we are seeing rumblings of revival in the most unlikely of places. There are reports that in places such as the Gaza Strip and Iraq, Muslims are knocking on the doors of churches every day asking for someone to tell them about the Jesus they saw in a dream or vision the night before. One young man who had his suicide bomb ready to detonate the next day had Jesus appear to him in a dream. As he sat up, a light moved back and forth in his room and continued the dialogue Jesus had begun with him in his dream. The man jumped out of his window, leaving everything behind for the next two years as he went in search of someone to tell him about Jesus. According to experts, Christianity is again the fastest-growing religion in the world. I believe we are on the cusp of the greatest move of God the world has ever seen.[1]

PROPHECY AND PRAYER

As happened with Daniel, it is hard to look at the Scriptures and events and not see that we are also in a prophetic age. As such, there is no more time for "business as usual" praying—prayers that essentially say, "Lord, make me healthy, wealthy, and wise." As the world has reached seven billion people and enters a time ever closer to the return of Christ, there is an urgent need for those who will pray as Daniel did, or like Anna, who "did not depart from the temple, but served God with fastings and prayers night and day" (Luke 2:37), praying she would see the Messiah before she died. We must hear from heaven and put God's plans into action on the earth. We must embrace the gospel to the full salvation of its hearers—not just solitary decisions for Christ, but lifetimes of decisions to follow Jesus each and every day. God mustn't find us sitting in bomb shelters waiting for the Rapture, but fervently working to expand His kingdom as the hour of His return draws near.

It is not enough to glimpse the kingdom in the distance and rush to slide under the gate just in time before it comes crashing down; we must press in and see the kingdom established wherever we go. Salvation is not a one-time decision that guarantees heaven, but it's a lifetime of releasing justice into our world on all levels. As Cornel West has repeatedly said, "Justice is what love looks like in public."[2] If we are going to live by Christ's commandment to love one another, justice is going to be our business at all levels. And nothing brings down justice like establishing the kingdom of God in a place.

I'm no doom-and-gloom preacher. I don't introduce the topic of Jesus' return to scare you or prophesy war and destruction over you. Certainly we know from Scripture that the Tribulation will be a very difficult time on the earth, and in leading up to it, the dark will get darker and the light will get lighter, but I want you who are part of the light to be among those who shine the brightest—at least that is what I plan to do! Where sin abounds, the Bible promises that grace will abound just that much more! (See Romans 5:20.)

In this age and generation each one of us has to be as engaged in prayer as Daniel was in his generation. Like Daniel, each one of us has been given industry-specific assignments, which can only be effectively and efficiently discharged once bathed in prayer. You have been planted in the workplace not just to earn a living but to superimpose, according to the law of life in Christ Jesus, over the law of sin and death, according to Romans 8:2. As God makes more of Himself available, those who hear from heaven best will be in on the most incredible things! We will accomplish great exploits in His name until the kingdoms of this world become the kingdom of our Lord and of His Christ—until He reigns forever and ever. I don't know about you, but I want to be right in the midst of what God is doing at that point on the earth. Just as Daniel, when he knew he was in a prophetic time, prayed and claimed God's promises, we must remind God of His Word and download God's plans and tactics and claim His promises for this generation.

As the day of the Lord draws nearer, we need to draw nearer to Him as well. It will be an exciting time to be on the earth, and I believe we are to get ready for it by doing our parts right where we are today. It is time to pray, fast, obey, and display the power of God. And that all starts with you digging in and fighting the battle you have right in front of you right now. Heaven already has the plans for your victory—it's time to download them and walk them out. Even as God protected Daniel and Joseph, so He will protect you. He will be with you when you are thrown into proverbial social and financial pits, cultural and corporate fiery furnaces, and political lions' den. He will place such distinction and favor upon you that your lifestyle and testimony will have the power to persuade your employers, employees, supervisors, and even government officials to proclaim:

> I make a decree that in every dominion of my kingdom men must tremble and fear before the God of Daniel. For He is the living God, and steadfast forever; His kingdom is the one which shall not be destroyed, and His dominion shall endure to the end. He delivers and rescues, and He works signs and wonders in heaven and on earth, who has delivered Daniel from the power of the lions.
>
> —DANIEL 6:26–27

Daniel's stand was an act that can be likened to Thoreau's civil disobedience and the nonviolence/passive resistance of Gandhi, Martin Luther King Jr., and Nelson Mandela. This is not a modern political strategy, because it can be traced back to Shiprah's and Puah's passive resistance against Pharaoh's abortion and Jewish Holocaust policies. As resistance fighters, understanding how powerful this posture is, is important because it is a deliberate, nonviolent refusal to conform to social, political, and cultural norms, laws, demands, traditions of a country, society, or government that undermines the Word of God. In one view (in India, known as *ahimsa* or *satyagraha*) it could be said that it is compassion expressed in the form of respectful disagreement. The Bible states that "love covers a multitude of sin" (1 Pet. 4:8, NAS). Love is stronger than death. This strategy has been used from one generation to another, from Gandhi's campaigns for independence from British rule to Czechoslovakia's Velvet Revolution to East Germany's oust of communist government to South Africa's fight against Apartheid to America's civil rights movement and recently in the Occupy Wall Street protests.

The Bible supports this philosophy because this is the strategy used by Jesus as He advanced the agenda of the kingdom. I believe that it worked because it is compassion driven, justice based, and biblically sound.

> Do not be conformed to this world, but be transformed by the renewing of your mind,

that you may prove what is that good and
acceptable and perfect will of God.

—ROMANS 12:2

When Jesus came, He came to establish the stone
kingdom. It is funny to think that God's progress
takes us back to the "stone age," not in the natural sense but the spiritual, because the stone that
the builders rejected became the chief cornerstone.
Jesus came in the fullness of time. God's time is
perfect, precise, and accurate. You have been born
at the right time and in the right generation. Your
presence in the earth is important. Your fulfillment
of your assignment should never be underestimated.

When Jesus came, Nebuchadnezzar's dream
had reached its crescendo. Rome had now become
the great political power in the earth. It was the
first government to keep people as indentured
laborers in their own country rather than taking
them to another country. They appointed gov-
ernors to rule over them. Israel—as well as the
Romans—expected that the king would take up
physical rule here, in the earth; hence their fear of
Jesus' proclamation that He was king and His trial
and subsequent execution after having been found
guilty of high treason.

For unto us a Child is born,
Unto us a Son is given;
And the government will be upon His
    shoulder.
And His name will be called
Wonderful, Counselor, Mighty God,
Everlasting Father, Prince of Peace.
Of the increase of His government and peace
There will be no end,
Upon the throne of David and over His
    kingdom,
To order it and establish it with judgment
    and justice
From that time forward, even forever.
The zeal of the LORD of hosts will perform
    this.

—ISAIAH 9:6–7

When Jesus came to this earth, His number one mission was to restore the government of God. This geopolitical mission was His highest priority and passion watered by prayer. He had three choices:

1. Acquiesce to the existing system, but He did not. He said in John 18:36, "My kingdom is not of this world."

2. Rebel and force the government to divest itself of its power, control, wealth, and resources for redistribution for the equitable treatment of all. He did not choose this option because He knew that God was the source of all His resources. He taught His disciples in Matthew 6:33: "Seek first the kingdom of God and His righteousness, and all these things shall be added to you."

3. Engage in civil disobedience against the Roman government. This was the option He chose as He taught His disciples how to give honor where honor was due in Matthew 22:21: "Render therefore to Caesar the things that are Caesar's, and to God the things that are God's." And as such, He constructed an alternative system—one that would bring peace, empowerment, prosperity, and an increase in the quality of life.

This meant that Jesus would engage in an initiative to sovereignly, cosmologically, and divinely reengineer the existing system by utilizing a strategy similar to that established by the Roman government. As the Romans conquered nation after nation and kingdom after kingdom, bringing them under its rule, governance, and dictatorship, they would announce the Romanization of the world through this phrase, "The Roman kingdom come and Caesar's will be done." Jesus' announcement of the establishment of His kingdom was: "Repent, for the kingdom of heaven is at hand" (Matt. 4:17).

The announcement of the kingdom was not a religious movement but a political one. Jesus was God's diplomat and ambassador sent with a mission and mandate as follows:

- Mission: destroy the works of the devil by establishing the kingdom.

- Mandate: redeem mankind and restore him back to:

- A right relationship with his Maker

- His position of power, jurisdictional authority, and dominion in the earth realm

Just as Daniel prospered through prayer—in spite of persecution and trials within his sphere of influence that drew the proverbial line in the sand of justice—and Jesus advanced the kingdom through deliberately living in such a way that His life transformed people, may you neither bow your knees to the god of this world nor compromise your convictions as God promotes and prospers you. Remember, as God makes you the head and not the tail—an industry leader, trendsetter, and an agent of change—and as you commit to develop a life of prayer, Scripture promises you:

> No temptation has overtaken you except such as is common to man; but God is faithful, who will not allow you to be tempted beyond what you are able, but with the temptation will also make the way of escape, that you may be able to bear it.
> —1 Corinthians 10:13

> The weapons of our warfare are not carnal but mighty in God.
> —2 Corinthians 10:4

> "No weapon formed against you shall prosper, and every tongue which rises against you in

judgment you shall condemn. This is the heritage of the servants of the LORD, and their righteousness is from Me," says the LORD.

—ISAIAH 54:17

Refuse to preserve the status quo.

❧ PART TWO ❧

PRAYER *on the* BATTLEFRONTS

The more the Christian is truly filled with the Spirit of Christ, the more spontaneous will be his giving himself up to the life of priestly intercession. Beloved fellow-Christians! God needs, greatly needs, priests who can draw near to Him, who live in His presence, and by their intercession draw down the blessings of His grace on others. And the world needs priests who will bear the burden of the perishing ones, and intercede on their behalf.[1]
—ANDREW MURRAY

Five

REVOLUTIONARY EMPOWERMENT

Keeping Others Down Costs Us All

Work as if everything depended upon your work, and
pray as if everything depended upon your prayer.
—WILLIAM BOOTH

If ever there comes a time when the women of the world
come together purely and simply for the benefit of mankind, it will be a force such as the world has never known.
—MATTHEW ARNOLD
Nineteenth-century British poet and philosopher

I DON'T DOUBT THAT you have heard the story of Esther many times and in many different settings. It is one of the most remarkable stories in the Bible. But I also think we forget some important things about the story because we get lost in the splendor of the palace, the court intrigue, and the eloquence of her cousin, Mordecai. I think if we recast it as a modern mobster movie—something like *The Departed*—it shows even more relevance to our times. After all, Ahasuerus (whom history knows better as Xerxes I, the son of Darius I) was little more than a mob boss and thug dressed up in royal robes.

Unhappy with his disobedient wife, he has her put away and promptly holds a beauty contest to replace her. Up out of the Jewish ghetto rises Esther, who wins the king's heart by her figure, purity, and looks. Esther was, in essence, a trophy wife. He pampered her and loved her, but it is hard to imagine they had much time to be together other than when he had her brought to his bedchamber. She was a kept girl, a girl who had to hide her heritage to do well, a girl who could be done away with by her husband simply snapping his fingers, just as he had done to his first wife.

Though Esther was a queen, the truth is she was little more than a wife dressed up in finer clothing and surroundings. The prenuptial agreement was solid; Esther would get nothing her husband didn't want her to have, and if she disturbed him when he was working, it could literally cost her, her head.

I know a lot of women who think they aren't of much importance because they are just a wife or mother—they don't work outside of the home, their relationship with their husband may be rocky, and they don't feel like they have much power or authority even over their own lives. If you have ever felt that way, I think you should read the story of Esther again in a new light. She was just like you. She could have shied away from the responsibility that came her way and simply sat back and kept house. But she didn't— because when she accessed the throne room, she changed the fate of a people. And the throne room she accessed was simply that of a nation, while we are told:

> Let us therefore come boldly to the throne
> of grace, that we may obtain mercy and find
> grace to help in time of need.
> —HEBREWS 4:16

The other side of Esther's story is, of course, that she was just a young woman thrust onto the public stage because of her beauty, and really for no other reason than she had something that pleased a very rich and powerful man. She was an *American Idol* winner, a Miss Persia, the singer who finally got the big contract, the talent that got noticed, the girl who married well. She landed an important place of popularity and fame in her society because of some God-given physical attribute. She could have let herself believe she was all that and a bag of chips, or she could use her position to influence the fate of her people.

Humility and godliness are more powerful than you can imagine. Take, for example, the testimony of Polly Wigglesworth. Her husband, Smith, was a plumber, and it was a season when work abounded for him and the money was flowing. Because of this he rarely went to church anymore and began to backslide in his faith. He even became jealous of the time Polly spent at church. One night when Polly came home later than usual, Smith got angry at her and said, "I am the master of this house, and I am not going to have you coming home at so late an hour as this." Polly, however, stood her ground and reminded her husband of her proper place. Quietly she said, "I know that you are my husband, but Christ is my master." At this Smith forced her out the back door and locked it behind her. Storming around the kitchen, he was surprised a few minutes later when she walked in from the front, laughing. He had forgotten to lock the front door to keep her out! Struck by both her mirth and the ridiculousness of the situation, Smith was soon laughing too. In this laughter with his wife Smith recognized the state of his heart and decided to spend the next ten days in prayer and fasting. In the years to come Smith Wigglesworth would go on to become one of the greatest healing evangelists the world has ever known, but had Polly not been faithful to the truth that night, would that have even happened? Had Esther not stood up as she did, what would have happened to the Jews?

I believe Esther is such a popular story because every woman can see a little bit of herself in Esther. We each, men and women alike, have a choice to make about wherever it is that God has placed us—about what we will do to influence heaven from right where we are.

Many believers are made to feel that somehow God cannot use them because they are "unequally yoked" (2 Cor. 6:14), but perhaps God has called you to influence the influencer in your life. Esther's assignment was critical because she had the ear of a decision-maker and policy-changer. Many of us are placed in these positions so that we can pray for divine counsel. Through prayer and fasting God gave Esther a plan to save her people and appointed Mordecai to give her counsel and wisdom. Then, even though it was very dangerous, she put it into action and saw her people not only saved but also completely delivered from their enemies. As you pray and fast, the Holy Spirit will counsel you and reveal to you His redemptive plan for your union. What is it that God is calling to you accomplish "for such a time as this" (Esther 4:14)?

The Value of a Life

The United Nations, as well as most development agencies around the world, has recognized in recent decades that if you want to lift a nation out of poverty, the most effective way is to empower its women. In the world's most developed nations, for example, women generally have a more equal standing with men. That is to say, women earn *roughly* the same pay for the same work, are involved in leadership both in business and politically, and are being educated in equal numbers with their male counterparts. In the poorest of the poor areas, projects that have turned women and mothers into entrepreneurs have done more to raise the standard of living in the community and the welfare of children than any others. There is an old saying: "If you give a man a fish, he will eat for a day. If you teach a man to fish, he will eat for a lifetime." But it appears, "If you teach a woman to fish, she will improve the quality of life for her entire community."

Now, if you are a man reading this, I am not trying

to come in on one side or the other about which gender is better or which should have authority over the other. We are told that, in the family, "the husband is head of the wife, as also Christ is head of the church" (Eph. 5:23). And:

> Husbands, love your wives, just as Christ also loved the church and gave Himself for her, that He might sanctify and cleanse her with the washing of water by the word, that He might present her to Himself a glorious church, not having spot or wrinkle or any such thing, but that she should be holy and without blemish. So husbands ought to love their own wives as their own bodies; he who loves his wife loves himself.
>
> —EPHESIANS 5:25–28

While a great deal has been preached about the "headship" of the husband, I think a great deal has also been overlooked regarding what these verses are actually saying. The analogy of a head and a body is not one of a top down hierarchy but that of cooperation between mind and heart, brain and physique. For example, is it possible for a head to stay seated on the coach watching football on TV while its body goes to get it a Coke from the fridge? Not if both parts are to stay alive! As we have already discussed to a small extent in the analogy of the church as the body of Christ, all the brainpower in the world is of little good unless the head and body are in sync acting as one. A smart head doesn't use and abuse its body to get what it wants; that would be a slow, demented form of suicide. Instead a head nurtures and cares for its body, for the success of the head and body are mutual. The body nourishes and oxygenates the head so that it can think, imagine, dream, see, and lead clearly. There is no success for either if they are not one.

Think for a moment of the analogy of Jesus Christ and the church. There is no success for Jesus on the earth without the success of the church. In fact, Jesus spends day and night at the right hand of the throne of God praying for the success of the church—that it would be delivered of those things that bind and hold it back, that oppress it; that it would realize the calling He has given to it and fully participate in realizing His dreams for each member. Jesus spends very little to no time trying to convince the body of His headship—His leadership is not His responsibility to enforce; it is up to the church to hear, recognize the truth of His vision for it, and obey. It is His part to determine to direct, instruct, and nurture; what the body does in response is up to the body. Jesus does not go to war with the body trying to get it to obey. Instead, He provides vision, provision, and leadership, and He loves the body into being all that it can be.

While the relationship between genders should be this way in marriage, it is not the same as brothers and sisters in Christ. As Paul put it in Galatians 3:26–28:

> For you are all sons [and daughters] of God through faith in Christ Jesus. For as many of you as were baptized into Christ have put on Christ. There is neither Jew nor Greek, there is neither slave nor free, there is no male and female, for you are all one in Christ Jesus.

If we are "one in Christ Jesus," that does not mean we are all the same, to be carbon copies of one another, but that we function as one body working together trying to maximize the effectiveness and success of each individual part. Leadership is shared just as menial work is shared. There is no longer "women's work" and "men's work," only "Jesus work." The church is an "all hands on deck" organization, and where anyone has a skill or an anointing, that person should be released by the rest of the body to do it to the glory of God, within the confines, of course, that they exhibit the proper character, compassion, and godliness. As Paul put it in Ephesians, we are to:

> Grow up in all things into Him who is the head—Christ—from whom the whole body, joined and knit together by what every joint supplies, according to the effective working by which every part does its share, causes growth of the body for the edifying of itself in love.
> —Ephesians 4:15–16

Now, before we get too far afield with this, let me tell you what my real point is. This is no redefinition of the roles of male and female within the church— I am trying to get back to the value of every individual who comes to Jesus no matter their gender, race, background, or socioeconomic status. What I am trying to do is get a "way of the world" out of the body of Christ and get us to do things the "kingdom of heaven way" instead.

The way of the world is to subjugate and control, divide and conquer, belittle and besmirch those who are not part of our group, ethnicity, race, religion, gender, political faction, or whatever—even "believer" and "nonbeliever" can be a slippery slope. Satan invented "us vs. them," not God. While there are "sheep and goats," so to speak, nothing in the Bible tells us it is up to us to separate them out unless they are preaching false doctrines or openly practicing sin in a way that is undermining themselves and the body of believers connected with them. We are, in fact, repeatedly told not to judge (Matt. 7:1; Luke 6:37; Rom. 14:13). Galatians 3:28 could as easily say, "There is neither Democrat or Republican; there is no white collar or blue collar; there is no black, brown, red, or beige," as well as any of the other lines we draw in the sand to divide one group from another. While there is unity in joining together with others to identify a heritage or who have similar ideologies, when such groups become divisions and cause power struggles, we are getting wrapped up in the way the enemy does things, not in God's ways.

What I am saying is that for those of us trying to live in the ways of the kingdom of God, using doctrine or tradition to hold one group of people down for the betterment of another is not God's method of operations. God is an empowerer. God wants to take the weak and lowly, the humble and meek, and see them exalted. If He brings down the proud, it is only because He wants to be the exalter and not see them exalt themselves to their own demise. His way is to maximize the potential of every person who will come to Him. He wants every person to become all she or he can be according to His original plan for each one.

If we are going to be like Him and make a difference on the earth, we need to operate in the same way. Men should not be looking to keep their wives under their control, but to see them grow and let them loose on the earth to be all God has called them to be. Women should not be jealous of the "ole boys' clubs" that are blamed for the glass ceilings in workplaces, but they should strive to establish God's goodness in that place—letting God bring down the walls as He did at Jericho. We, men and women, are supposed to have the attitudes of servants toward one another, lifting each other up and edifying one another. Respect and authority flow from our being more like Jesus, not in us clutching to our titles and positions as those in the world do or using oppressive stereotypes to promote ourselves.

With that in mind, we have to be the champions of those who are downtrodden, oppressed, and exploited. Jesus died that all might be free; we need to live for the same. We need to pray into these areas, and then act on what God is telling us to do in them. If there is a member of the opposite sex or another racial group we feel is putting stumbling blocks between who we are now and who God wants to be, we are told to pray for them, not to complain about them. If we really want to attack poverty and infant mortality, and spur growth in developing nations, research points to improving the position of women in those nations as one of the fastest and most effective ways to accomplish those goals. This is not a matter of women's rights as the world preaches it, but it is a matter of lifting up the downtrodden for the betterment of all. After all, "Pure and undefiled religion before God and the Father is this: to visit orphans and widows in their trouble, and to keep oneself unspotted from the world" (James 1:27). I have to believe this only echoes the call to "preach the gospel to the poor," "to heal the brokenhearted," and "to set at liberty those who are oppressed" (Luke 4:18), as Jesus announced His mission to be.

CHANGING MIND-SETS

Perhaps a better way to illustrate this is by telling a simple story typical of the plight of young women in underdeveloped countries. One such story is that of Kakenya.[1]

Kakenya was a young girl in a poor African village.

Her parents arranged for her to be married when she was only five, something typical for her culture. In her village, when a girl is old enough to walk, she is taught how to sweep the house, collect water from the river, and cook for her family. Girls are trained to be mothers, and boys are trained to be warriors. It is a cycle that reinforces a lifestyle that is no longer functional and keeps the village living as it did centuries before rather than allowing for progress. It also dictates a very hard life for everyone.

Kakenya, however, wanted something more. She wanted to be a teacher. Her parents told her that if she finished her chores each day, she could go to school, so Kakenya worked hard every morning to finish early and go to school.

In this village, when girls are around twelve or thirteen years old, they go through a ceremony they are told makes them a woman. They are told they must not cry during this ceremony. Once they are women, they can get married, and going to school quickly falls from the options of a teenager who has a husband to take care of and soon becomes a mother.

Kakenya went to her father and convinced him to let her finish secondary school before he forced her to marry, and after some time, he agreed. Then, when she was nearing graduation, she wanted to go to college so that she could fulfill her dream of becoming a teacher. However, her father was very sick, so he had no means to send her.

In her culture, when a father becomes sick, it is the responsibility of all the other men of his age in the community to become his children's fathers. Furthermore, the tribe had a custom that anyone who comes to you before the sun rises is a bearer of good news, and therefore you must not tell them no. So, systematically, Kakenya got up early and went to the men of the village before sunrise one by one. Finally, when all of the elders had agreed, they pooled their money and sent Kakenya to university. She was the first girl from the village to go to college.

Kakenya worked hard and eventually earned a PhD. With it she returned to her village and helped build a primary school where girls could go, dream, and escape the cycle of poverty that Kakenya had only just managed to outwit. It would mean huge strides forward for the entire village.

No nation that overburdens a major talent pool can ever reach its full potential. With women making up half of any culture's population, they represent a large talent pool that should be empowered to bring into the world what God has put into them. This doesn't mean women shouldn't be housewives and mothers—for that is an enormously important role—but that women should have the freedom to become all who God has called them to be.

In areas where women are still subjugated, in many countries as second-class citizens, where they are limited to working in agriculture or menial labor, families and societies suffer. Meanwhile barbaric customs such as female genital mutilation are still practiced as a means of enslaving women in far too many nations. When minds are tapped that have previously been subjugated, overworked, and ignored, the effect is not one of addition, but one of exponential multiplication. When women are empowered, new products become available that push into new markets, bring new money into communities, and raise the standards and availability of jobs for villages and towns. New networks are created, and ideas that needed each other to succeed have a better chance to meet one another and create further breakthroughs. Education, medical care, and participating in the political process all receive new financing and focus.

The world needs a radical new equilibrium between its citizens—one that empowers each to be all that he or she can be rather than one that exploits or tries to control them. While women may be the largest group to benefit from this, it also means radical new relationships between races, ethnic groups, religions, and political parties. There will always be differences, but if we embrace diversity instead of avoid it—nurture and learn from one another rather than control and compete for power—those differences will enrich us and make us healthier and wiser overall.

Our workplaces, school grounds, and university campuses are filled with souls crying out for help, hope, solutions, and salvation. You must engage in the redemptive power of prayer continuously. Be open to the prompting of the Spirit of God as He directs you to pray for specific individuals and their needs. It is possible that your assignment may not be limited to just praying for individual needs. You may be the answer to the very prayers that you are praying. Prayer is truly a lifesaving activity. There is no community, no nation, no organization, no city, no government, no child, no marriage, and no personal condition that is off limits to its impact. There is no power, policy, or principality on earth that can prohibit or prevent prayer from working. Prayer is a mountain mover. Do not be discouraged if it appears as if your prayers are not working as quickly as you anticipated. Never give up on anyone. One day George Müller began praying for five of his friends. After many months one of them came to the Lord. Ten years later two others were converted. It took twenty-five years before the fourth man was saved. Müller persevered in prayer until his death for the fifth friend, and throughout those fifty-two years he never gave up hoping that he would accept Christ! His faith was rewarded, for soon after Müller's funeral, the last one was saved. Let this story encourage you to persevere in prayer.

To that end remember to pray for those who would spitefully use or abuse other people. (See Matthew 5:44.) Pray the Ephesians prayers for them that they would have their eyes open to who God is and the depth and breadth of all the dimensions of His love. When you do, you open up new possibilities not only for yourself but also for everyone else in the world. We need to tie our success to the success of all—for when the water table rises, we all rise with it.

Six

DELIVERING *the* CAPTIVES

Breaking the Bonds of Exploitation,
Oppression, and Abuse

Wherever faith has accepted the Father's love, obedience
accepts the Father's will. The surrender to, and the prayer for
a life of heaven-like obedience, is the spirit of childlike prayer.[1]
—ANDREW MURRAY

D ESPITE GROWING UP on the mission field,
Shelley Hundley entered college—a Christian college, in fact—as a hostile, out-
spoken atheist. Being abused as a child by another
missionary while living in Medellín, Colombia, one
of the most violent and dangerous cities in the world,
Shelley became convinced that God could not exist
if such atrocities happened so regularly with no
repercussions. If there was no justice, there was no
God. The abuse of her past had so disturbed her that

she had suppressed the memories. A meeting with someone who had been on the mission field with her parents brought out some of the facts about other children who had been abused—some of whom had been her friends—and suddenly the memories started to surface with incredible pain and feelings of self-loathing and worthlessness. It was this that sparked Shelley's conviction that there was no God—and her determination to put an end to her life.

Shelley's story is heartbreaking enough as it illustrates the trauma and pain one human being can perpetrate upon another, but her turnaround is even more remarkable for what it shows of the grace and mercy of God. As she was on her way to the roof of her dorm to throw herself off, someone miraculously intervened, and Shelley ended up in a padded safe room in a local medical facility where she couldn't hurt herself. Sitting in that room, literally at the end of her rope, Shelley lifted up a simple prayer to the God she didn't believe in:

> If there is a God who can hear me, if there is a God who can see me right now in the state I'm in, if You want me to live, You have to give me two things, or I cannot continue. I won't go on this way.

First, you have to prove to me beyond any doubt, just between You and me, that You are real. I can't take anyone else's word for it again. Second, if You prove Yourself to me, knowing that You exist is not enough. You have to show me that You can do something about this pain. Otherwise I vow right now that I will not live this way, and I will end my life the next chance I get.[2]

Despite not giving an immediate response, God heard Shelley's prayer, and a powerful set of circumstances went into action. As a group on campus continued to pray for her, things got worse for Shelley. She was released from the hospital after ten days, but something in the cafeteria a few days later triggered the most horrifying memories she had experienced to date, and Shelley went into such traumatic shock when she returned to her room that she became catatonic, lying frozen on her bed and staring into space. Over the next few days friends and counselors helped her come out of this, but the desire to kill herself returned stronger than ever, and she was again hospitalized. All the while students continued to pray and fast, asking for her salvation.

Being away from school so much took a toll on

Shelley's assignments and grades, so she spent a lot of time talking with professors when she was again released. Most of her professors seemed to have given up on her, but not her history professor. One afternoon when he called her, she was sure he was going to ask about a paper that was due or test her poor excuse for missing class that week, but instead he said, "Shelley, I was praying this morning and preparing for the Saturday night Bible study I lead at my house each week, and God spoke to me....God told me that you are to come tonight. God is going to heal your body and touch your heart."[3] Shelley felt that was the last place on earth she ever wanted to be, but for some mysterious reason, she found herself agreeing to go. Determined to keep her word, she showed up at the very end so she could get out quickly. But she didn't understand the type of Bible study she was walking into. Instead of ending when the clock said it was time to go—they continued until God was done with what He wanted to do. Telling her friend to wait in the car, Shelley planned to walk in, nod to her professor, and then make a break for it.

When she walked in, the group was closing in worship. She had never seen people so into singing, raising their hands, eyes closed, pouring their souls out to God. As soon as she made eye contact with her professor, he quieted the worship leaders and announced she was there. The group immediately surrounded her in loving attention. "Shelley, can we pray for you?" the professor asked. Not sure what he meant, she replied, "Yes. Sure, pray for me." The professor placed a chair in the center of the room and asked her to sit down. She wasn't sure why, but she again found herself agreeing and obeying. This was unlike anything she had ever experienced growing up in church or on the mission field. Uncomfortable with being touched by others, Shelley was shocked when the entire group laid their hands on her from her head all the way down to her shoes. She tensed and closed her eyes, saying to herself, "God, if you exist at all, You had better reveal Yourself now because I will never humiliate myself like this again." It proved to be all the opening Jesus needed.

A weighty presence immediately descended on Shelley, and she lost all sense of what was happening around her. It was as if she was in the room alone with God. As she described it, "Every fiber of my being knew that He was real, that He was present, and that He could do whatever He wanted with me.... It was terrifying and enthralling all at once."[4]

When this sensation began to slowly lift, Shelley became aware of those around her. As she did, she heard them saying things about her childhood she had never told anyone. Her self-loathing and shame began to crumble under the weight of the love she felt from the group and the words they spoke to her straight from the Father's heart. The girl who knelt before her with her hands on her shoes—a girl Shelley had verbally abused several times and to whom she had never been anything but rude—began sobbing uncontrollably. Rising up she put her forehead to Shelley's, but the words didn't seem to want to come as she tried to speak. "It's just that…it's just that…" She stammered and sobbed. "It's just that…it's just that…He loves you so much!"

In that instant, though she couldn't grasp it with her mind even by half, Shelley suddenly realized there was something worth living for—knowing the love of God like this girl knew the love of God. She determined at that moment to do whatever it took to experience the reality and depth of that love for herself. And, yes, God could do something about her pain. In the coming weeks Shelley would move through stages of recovery it normally took people years to experience. The transformation that began in Shelley's life in that meeting continues today as she works with Mike Bickle and the rest of the staff as a teacher and intercessor at the International House of Prayer in Kansas City, Missouri.

In praying for healing for her past and for others who had experienced similar abuse, God revealed Himself to Shelley in a way that we in modern society have all but forgotten—as the just God who will fight for His children against all who would harm or misuse them. It was a revelation of God as judge, but not the judge who is looking to pounce on us whenever we do something wrong; God is the righteous judge who will vindicate His beloved children and who will radically bring His justice down on persecutors. It is one of the most powerful revelations of who God is that I have ever read. I would encourage you to get her book, *A Cry for Justice*, and read it to get the full impact of what God has shown her. Jesus not only loves us, but He is also the righteous judge who fights for the oppressed, abused, and exploited. There is both deliverance and justice in knowing Christ as our righteous judge and in knowing He stands with us when we hand our cares, hurts, and anxieties over to Him.

WHEN JUSTICE ROLLS DOWN LIKE WATERS, AND RIGHTEOUSNESS LIKE A MIGHTY STREAM

Today we live in a world with more men, women, and children enslaved than were ever taken out of Africa. It is estimated that there are now as many as 35 million slaves on the earth, and the biggest portion of them are being sexually trafficked. Syndicates sell drugs, arms, and human beings as the three most profitable commodities, destroying millions more in the process. Meanwhile, in homes across America unspeakable acts of violence and abuse are perpetrated on the most innocent. It even happens in our churches! Pedophiles abuse several victims before any steps are taken to expose their iniquities.

Oppression is not only against individuals. Around the world Christians are attacked in the streets, as well as in their churches, for their beliefs. Recently in Nigeria a church was firebombed and church members were murdered with machine guns as they ran from the flames. Other believers sit in prisons around the world because they acknowledge Jesus as the only way to heaven—some are even on death row. Such things ought not to be.

We need a judge to step in and make things right.

Yet at the same time we need to realize that the cross was the ultimate judgment for all people. When the early Christians prayed for Saul the persecutor who was trying to crush the early church, God visited him with justice, and Saul became Paul the apostle. God turned darkness into light. When Shelley Hundley finally met her abuser face-to-face years after she had given her life to God, she had already prayed through what the man had done to her and forgiven him beyond anything the world might imagine. When she looked on him, she saw him as God saw him, a broken and corrupted man whom Jesus had died for just as much as He had died for anyone else. She prayed that her abuser's eyes would be open to who God is and how much He loved him. Should he accept that love and let it transform him, God could radically heal him as well; but if he refuses, justice will take a very different course. There is a reason the Bible tells us that the fear of God is the beginning of wisdom, for there is much to fear about such an awesome God who will not let the blood of His martyrs or the stolen innocence of His children go without retribution.

Even the earth itself groans with earthquakes and calamities hoping for righteousness to be established on the earth. The world was not built as a place that could handle the corruption that comes from sin. As things grow darker, the earth cries out all the more for the justice of God to be established. As Paul tells us in Romans:

> For the creation was subjected to futility, not willingly, but because of Him who subjected it in hope; because the creation itself also will be delivered from the bondage of corruption into the glorious liberty of the children of God. For we know that the whole creation groans and labors with birth pangs together until now.
> —ROMANS 8:20–22

Thus, as the world grows darker near the end of the current age, the earth will groan all the more with uprisings and calamities as we have already seen from Hurricane Katrina to the earthquakes in Haiti to the tsunami that hit Japan. Such things, however, are like the rain that falls on the just and unjust. (See Matthew 5:45.) They do not hit these places because the "wrath of God" is falling, but because the earth is groaning from the corruption of sin. It is not hitting specific areas because of their sinfulness, but coming aground devastating the righteous and unrighteous alike. There was no intercessor to stand in the gap before these things happened—there was no prophet who alerted those who pray to the need for more diligent prayer to avert such catastrophes. This is why we need to pray until we can *really* pray. We need to dig into God preemptively so God thinks of us before any new event hits the earth.

This is exactly what happened when Abraham prayed for Sodom and Gomorrah in Genesis 18. God knew Abraham as His covenant partner on the earth—His *friend*. When He knew Sodom and Gomorrah had to be judged or their evil would overrun the earth, He said to Himself:

> Shall I hide from Abraham what I am doing, since Abraham shall surely become a great and mighty nation, and all the nations of the earth shall be blessed in him? For I have known him, in order that he may command his children and his household after him, that they keep the way of the Lord, to do righteousness and justice, that the Lord may bring to Abraham what He has spoken to him.
>
> —Genesis 18:17–19

Considering this, He decided to double-check to see if things were actually as bad as they seemed, and in the process He alerted Abraham to the plight of the two cities. Knowing the nature of God as he did, Abraham began to reason with God from the perspective of God's nature. Would He destroy the righteous with the unrighteous? Just how many righteous people do there need to be to save the city? Fifty? Forty-five? Forty? Thirty? Twenty? Ten? Finally God conceded, "I will not destroy it for the sake of ten" (v. 32). Abraham, confident that his nephew Lot would at least have converted a dozen or so to live righteously by now, left it at that. Had he pushed farther, he might have been able to persuade God to spare the city for Lot's sake alone, but in the end, when only Lot and his family were found to be righteous, God saved them while the metropolises of Sodom and Gomorrah were destroyed.

We see that God will spare a city or even an entire nation for the sake of one faithful soul who will stand in the gap on their behalf. In Exodus 32 God is so fed up with the sinfulness of the children of Abraham whom He has delivered from Egypt, He is ready to wipe them all out and restart the nation of Israel from Moses alone. But Moses, knowing this is not God's true nature, began to reason together with God searching for a different option.

> Then Moses pleaded with the LORD his God, and said: "LORD, why does Your wrath burn

hot against Your people whom You have brought out of the land of Egypt with great power and with a mighty hand? Why should the Egyptians speak, and say, 'He brought them out to harm them, to kill them in the mountains, and to consume them from the face of the earth'? Turn from Your fierce wrath, and relent from this harm to Your people. Remember Abraham, Isaac, and Israel, Your servants, to whom You swore by Your own self, and said to them, 'I will multiply your descendants as the stars of heaven; and all this land that I have spoken of I give to your descendants, and they shall inherit it forever.'" So the LORD relented from the harm which He said He would do to His people.

—EXODUS 32:11–14

Scripture tells us:

Surely the Lord GOD does nothing, unless He reveals His secret to His servants the prophets.
—AMOS 3:7

In our age, that means God is looking for those on earth who are listening for heaven's instructions on what needs to be prayed for, who needs to be interceded for, and what needs to be prayed away before it happens. When there is no intercessor willing to stand in the gap and pray until heaven's righteousness can overcome the earth's corruption—legally according to the Word of God—chaos reigns and lives are destroyed in war, pestilence, famine, and/or natural disasters.

While we have seen the devastation that such things can inflict, only heaven knows how many others have been prevented by prayer. God's first course of justice is always grace, but if there is no repentance or acceptance of that grace, what happens next is rarely pretty. Sin has always cost blood to atone for it, and if we do not plead the blood of Jesus over a situation, then the ramifications are always dire, whether it be for an individual or a country.

On the other hand, who knows how many generations could be saved from one night spent on our knees praying as heaven directs? Israel was saved because of Moses's prayer—how many who live today would never have been had the generation been lost? And what of the offspring of Lot and his family? Out of Lot's lineage came the people of Moab, and Ruth was a Moabite. Ruth became the great-grandmother of David and one of those listed in the genealogy of Jesus Himself. Had it not been for Abraham's prayer generations before, where would Ruth have been? It is hard to say, but God would have been forced to bring the Messiah to the earth through a different lineage. This is no absolute, but it is an illustration of how one prayer can change the destiny of people generations later. Your faithfulness to pray as heaven directs today *will* have eternal consequences, even if you never see the ramifications of your prayers in your lifetime.

I know this is true in my own life. When I was a young girl living in poverty, my mother showed me a letter from a former neighbor that said she was praying for our family and each of us children specifically. My life is still impacted today from prayers made by a lady I never knew. Although she has passed away, her prayers are still prevailing. I believe that it was partially her prayers that birthed me out of poverty.

I can think of many nations that we are praying for today from Liberia to Kenya, Morocco to Brazil, North Korea to the Netherlands, Russia to Patagonia, Israel to Ireland, Canada to Chile, that we may never physically visit, but we can spiritually help. As we pray for those people today, what will be birthed from those places? What great leaders, what great scientists, what great inventors, what great men and women of God will emerge from those places because of our prayers? Not only is heaven counting on our prayers, but it is also very likely that so is someone out there we will never even know existed until the day they come up to us in heaven and thank us for praying that specific hour on that specific day. I may not know everything there is about prayer, but this one thing I do know—God answers prayer.

CASTING OUR CARES

Paul tells us in Ephesians:

> For we do not wrestle against flesh and blood, but against principalities, against powers, against the rulers of the darkness of this age, against spiritual hosts of wickedness in the heavenly places.
> —EPHESIANS 6:12

We need to realize, as Shelley did, that we are not responsible to "inflict" justice on our world, but to give it into the hands of Jesus in prayer and then do as He instructs us. We must take out evil at its roots, which is in the spiritual realm, and then act on that victory in the natural.

Again, William and Catherine Booth's work with The Salvation Army is a great example of balancing the work of the physical with the spiritual to attack the social issues of their time. They called for regular "knee drills" at every post of the Army, bathing every activity and action in fervent prayer. They were so adamant about this, that once when recruits were sent to a new area and reported they were failing to reach anyone, General Booth sent back a simple two-word telegram: "Try tears." When they called out to God all that much more intensely, a new post for The Salvation Army was established in that town.

At the same time they did what they could in the natural and wrote out their plans to take people out of poverty. They believed that you could not save the soul of a man or woman whose stomach growled through the preaching of the gospel and at the same time refused to take away the dignity of anyone by giving them handouts. People who needed shelter could find it for a very low fee or else would be given work to earn their keep. They fought and lobbied for better working conditions in factories, helped people retrain themselves for new jobs, carried out an elaborate plan to raise the age of consent in Great Britain and end child prostitution, as well as a multitude of endeavors God led them to attempt. They accomplished a great deal in only a handful of decades by going to the lowest of the low and empowering them to be all they could be in Christ.

In a world of seven billion and with societies drunk on entertaining themselves or fulfilling their darkest desires, many of the ills that organizations like The Salvation Army helped minimize have come back with great force today. We must combat them in prayer and action. We must protest them in the halls of government and the halls of heaven. We must get a greater revelation of Jesus as judge and deeper understandings and insight into both the fear of the Lord and the agape love of God, which takes us right back to Paul's prayers for the Ephesians.

While prayer is first and foremost connecting with God, it is also influencing heaven for the sake of the earth and downloading kingdom plans for the salvation and redemption of earth's citizens. Becoming as passionate as the abolitionists of old and those who marched with Dr. King should only fuel our prayers all the more. It is time to set aside even more of the distractions of this world for the sake of understanding kingdom ways and wearing thin the veil between heaven and earth. If not us who feel it most intensely and have the ear of heaven as our inheritance, then who?

Seven

RADICAL ECONOMICS

Understanding True Riches and the Purpose of Money

> The first and primary object of the work was, (and still
> is) that God might be magnified by the fact, that the
> orphans under my care are provided, with all they
> need, only by prayer and faith, without any one being
> asked by me or my fellow-laborers, whereby it may be
> seen, that God is faithful still, and hears prayer still.[1]
> —GEORGE MÜLLER

THE FINANCIAL MELTDOWN of 2008 rocked the stability of the world's system of financing to its core and increased the gap between rich and poor the world over. Doctrines of deregulation for the securities and investment banking industries that started in the Reagan years and were compounded by Presidents Clinton and Bush "freed" Wall Street from investing to spur industry to gambling with people's retirement savings. They hoped they wouldn't be the last ones holding the hot potatoes of derivatives and CDOs that in the end proved little more than worthless promises on paper. Telling Congress that Adam Smith's "invisible hand"—a concept Smith only mentioned once in all of his writings—would always keep the economy in equilibrium, Wall Street spent billions to get votes to free their greed to grab all they could before the bubble burst.

In the 1980s Wall Street was only responsible for about 15 percent of all the corporate profit in the United States. They provided speculative money to companies that developed products that could make life easier and more comfortable. This type of speculation and investment banking was carefully quarantined from the rest of the US economy, so if it should get out of control, only its own investors would suffer while the rest of the economy remained unaffected. Because of the lessons we learned from the Great Depression, safeguards were built into law that would keep something that devastating from ever happening again.

However, after decades of relatively regular and slow but steady growth, people started to believe we had grown too wise to repeat the mistakes of the past. In 1972, in the hope of jump-starting a stubborn economy, Richard Nixon took the United

States off of the gold standard—something that got him a quick boost in the polls and reelection in 1972 in the greatest landslide vote ever, but it ultimately opened the door to the stagflation that rocked the nation in the decades to come.

In the 1980s, in the hope of spurring the economy, the Reagan administration loosened the regulations on Wall Street and banking. As a result the United States experienced the greatest one-day drop in the history of the stock market on Black Monday in 1988—and the savings and loan scandals that looted the savings of a great many Americans. The bolts to the wheels that Reagan loosened, Bill Clinton all but took out, and George W. Bush did nothing to correct. As a result we experienced the Internet bubble of the late 1990s and the eventual recession of 2008, each crash dwarfing the one before. In the months before the crash of 2008, the investment banking industry had reached a height of being responsible for 41 percent of the corporate profits in the United States—an industry that didn't make cars, refrigerators, or even tanks and fighter planes, but one that traded promises on paper. When those promises proved worthless, the bottom fell out, and to save the economy, the government footed the bill to the tune of trillions of dollars. A tsunami of unemployment circled the planet, wiping out the livelihoods of millions, but Wall Street investment bankers—the very ones responsible for the catastrophe—still got their seven-figure bonuses. Some, of course, lost their jobs, something that gave them millions again in severance packages, and they dropped out of investment banking and got into things such as university teaching and advising President Obama on economic policy.

I don't have the space or really the background to get into all of that here, but the long and the short of it is, except for a large influx of cash from the government, nothing has really changed in the investment banking industry. Laws have not been changed, Congress has had to extend the debt ceiling repeatedly to keep up with its expenses, and there is more division and divisive rhetoric on Capitol Hill than any of us have experienced in our lifetimes. The world is heading toward another bubble if things don't change soon, and this time the economy won't have the reserves to right itself again. Instead of banks, it will be governments that take the brunt of the collapse. It might be something we can prolong beyond our lifetimes, but it could also be something that happens in just a handful of years.

Regardless, the time is now for us to learn

revolutionary new ways to live based on revolutionary new ways to interact with money. The Bible tells us that, "The borrower is servant to the lender" (Prov. 22:7), and Jesus told us, "You cannot serve God and mammon [the spirit of wealth]" (Matt. 6:24). We must pray and decide: Will we master money, or will money be the master of us? On the basis of that decision lies the economy of the kingdom of God versus being subject to the kingdom of this world.

BY PRAYER ALONE

In my book *The Prayer Warrior's Way* we looked briefly at the life of George Müller and the revolutionary way in which he financed his ministry to orphans in the late 1800s. He took the stand early in his ministry that he would never ask anyone for money, never give a call for an offering when he spoke, and never pass the plate at a meeting. Instead he would ask God to meet his needs and those of what God called him to do. By the end of his life George was running a ministry that housed, clothed, and daily fed over 2,000 orphans without George asking anyone but God for money. If such a thing can happen to an uneducated fellow in the middle of the nineteenth century—who by the end of his life cared for over 10,000 orphans and educated over 120,000 children—certainly we in the twenty-first century can learn to relate in radically different ways to money, if we could but learn to pray in faith as Müller did.

Of course, that type of world-shattering paradigm isn't established overnight—but if we are consistently applying the prayer principles we have discussed throughout the Art of War series, then turning ourselves to trust God for finances shouldn't be a stretch. While I don't believe we have to be as extreme as George Müller, his example is a shining lesson of what is possible through prayer alone.

We must take those principles and apply them to the crisis that is before us—and it may not be helping orphans, but chances are it will demand some kind of financial component, whether it be just in your own household, in the company you work for, in your church, in the nonprofit where you volunteer, or in the company you own or the business you are about to start. Understanding how you use money—how to make it your servant—will likely be crucial to the success of your enterprise—whatever that may be—while letting it run rampant and letting it control you could well capsize your God-given dream.

There is so much out there on good, biblical financial wisdom from people such as Larry Burkett and

Dave Ramsey that I urge you to use the resources they provide as a great place to begin. Listen to Dave Ramsey's shows or podcasts regularly to train your mind to think biblically when it comes to finances. Learn to discipline your personal spending habits and working habits according to their advice and the Book of Proverbs. Learn to see money as a tool and not a reward. Let truth transform your relationship with money to the point that your job is not a means of paying your bills as much as an expression of the purpose God has for your life. If it's not, then you'll either need to change your mind-set or your job. Again, God will lead you as you seek Him for His guidance.

At the same time we need to learn to think bigger. The world's mind-set over macro- and micro-economics has created the mess we are currently in, and there appears little evidence it will change without major policy changes in the United States and the European Union. But we also need business owners who run companies based on biblical finances, who will provide for their employees as someone who cares for their welfare as much as their own. We need innovators who will create the breakthrough products that will transform industries and then be the influencers to communicate a kingdom finance mind-set to replace the greed that is presently corrupting the world system. We need kingdom expanders, not personal empire builders. Someone has to rise up with those new ideas—why not someone in the body of Christ? Why not you?

When Joseph was finally released from prison, it was not his ability to interpret dreams that got him the job as prime minister, but it was his financial wisdom. When Pharaoh was dumbfounded for what to do during the seven years of famine, Joseph already had a plan for what to do during the seven years of abundance. By not eating the surplus in the good years and storing it away safely, they would have more than enough when the bad years came.

In essence, what Joseph did was buy a fifth (20/80—the reverse of Pareto's 80/20 theory) of all the grain made available during each of the plentiful years—when no one would miss the surplus he was buying and prices were low because there was so much. However, when the famine hit and grain was nowhere to be found, Joseph could sell it back at whatever price he wanted because he had a monopoly on grain. During the seven years of plenty Egypt prospered because they had more than enough. Joseph, on the other hand, lived moderately and used the extra cash to buy more grain.

Then when the famine hit, it was time for Joseph

to sell. During the seven years of famine, everything of value that could be bought, Joseph traded grain for. At the end of seven years the crown owned everything in Egypt, including the land, animals, and people—everything but what the priests owned because they were independent of the crown. Joseph then sharecropped the land and animals back to the farmers, setting up a system by which the crown would always be provided for. God has His own economic stimulus package for every believer if we would but press in and pray to receive it.

Those who can learn from the story of Joseph understand that doing the opposite of the rest of the society financially are often the ones who end up wealthy in the end. When money is good, most people would spend it, but Joseph saved. When everyone was selling, Joseph was buying. Then, when everyone else was buying, Joseph was selling. At the end of fourteen years, which is far short of a lifetime, Joseph went from having nothing but the clothes on his back to controlling almost everything in Egypt. If you add to that a charitable spirit, imagine the good he could suddenly do. As it was, his ingenuity saved the entire Middle East from starving to death. It was quite a feat, even just at that.

In the financial craziness that formed the

housing bubble, those banks that were saving and staying out of the frenzy of buying and selling derivatives now own most of the banks that were in the midst of causing the crisis. If you had cash to buy a house in 2009, you would have gotten almost twice the house for your money than at the beginning of 2008. Those who are patient, who understand the up-and-down cycles of any economy, and who exercise wisdom as Joseph did will prosper in unexpected ways. And when they do, they will have great power to do good.

WHO NEEDS MONEY?

When we look at prophecy, we learn that some day in the future the following cry will be heard in the marketplaces of the world:

> A quart of wheat for a denarius [a day's wages],
> and three quarts of barley for a denarius; and
> do not harm the oil and the wine.
> —REVELATION 6:6

By today's standards that would mean a quart of wheat or three quarts of barley would go for about $240. The oil and wine would be so expensive, traders would tell common buyers to stay far clear of them so they would remain unharmed. This could only be describing a time such as Germany experienced after World War I.

After losing the First World War and getting stuck by the other European nations to pay their expenses for having to participate in it, the German government had the bright idea that the way to get out of trouble was to print the money they needed to pay all their bills and salaries. With the other European countries demanding the war debt be paid in gold equivalents, Germany went mad trying to stimulate its economy by spending new money. The effect was minimal at first, but in 1923, when people had to empty their bank accounts to keep up and all the money available flooded into the market places, Germany experienced hyperinflation. The German mark literally lost half its value each month. Starting in 1923, the mark was roughly 18,000 to the dollar (in June of 1921, it had been 60 marks to the dollar), but by the end of the year it took 4.2 billion marks to buy one dollar! People took wheelbarrows of cash to the store to buy bread. Others burned bundles of marks to heat their homes because it was cheaper than trying to buy firewood. Mobs descended on farms and slaughtered animals on the spot in order to get food to feed their families. It was a time of great unrest, and the bitterness that formed during those days was exactly what the National Socialist (Nazi) Party needed to rise to power. Playing the political blame game, the Nazis turned prejudice and resentment into votes, and then turned that power into attempted genocide and world war.

I don't believe that anything we see in the end times will be something we haven't already seen in history. Jesus described the signs of the end times as "birth pangs" (Matt. 24:8, NAS), meaning they will start slowly and distinctly, then come faster and more intense as the time of fulfillment comes. I think we are seeing that with economics. We are heading for the day when a loaf of bread will sell for hundreds of dollars and most common goods will be so expensive that no one but the richest of the rich will be able to buy them.

While I hope that by that time we will already be with Jesus enjoying the marriage supper of the Lamb, it could be we will see the day when money is no longer worth anything. On that day those with faith who can receive from God through prayer will be of infinite worth. God fed Israel in the desert with manna and quail (Exod. 16) and had ravens bring Elijah his meals (1 Kings 17:6). If we have faith in God, do we really have to depend upon money? It seems to me we need to be a little more open-minded. If we are to fully trust God for what we need, we need to ask for it directly and not be caught in the trap that the only answer is more money.

What the future holds for those who belong to God is full of promise. If we live in a time where sin abounds, then we are promised that the grace of God—His virtuous power that fills in for whatever we lack—will all that much more abound. If the world exists in a time of catastrophe, then we will live in a time of miracles. The revival we are about to experience before the week of tribulation will be mind-blowing! And chances are, we will be part of it.

To succeed in such a time, we must be people of faith who have been trained in prayer and see God as the source of our resources. There won't be any margin to go back and create years of experience of seeking and hearing God. We will need to have already done that. We need to exercise our faith every day, even if it is just for a parking spot. The Bible tells us that "the just shall live by faith" (Rom. 1:17). It doesn't say "by money" or "because they have the best jobs," but "by faith." We must cultivate that kind of faith for everyday living, and the best way to do that is by constantly being in prayer and trusting God to give us the answer—even when easier natural means are available. It was a faith George Müller showed us was possible. Let us be open to the same radical provision he was!

Eight

In STEP *With the* SPIRIT

*The Power of Bottom-to-Top
Integrity in Every Aspect of Life*

Prayer in this [Jesus'] name gets answers. The Moravians
prayed—the greatest revival till that time hit the world.
Finney prayed—America rocked with the power. Hudson
Taylor prayed—China's Inland Mission was born. Evan
Roberts prayed seven years—the Welsh revival resulted....

Seymour [of Azusa] prayed five hours a day for three and one-
half years. He prayed seven hours a day for two and one-half
years more. Heaven's fire fell over the world, and the most
extensive revival of real religion in this century resulted.[1]

—JOHN G. LAKE

C HARLES COLSON WAS known as Richard
Nixon's "hatchet man." That meant if something needed to be done, no matter the
nature of its ethics, Colson was the man who would
get it done. If you needed insider information to

implicate the other party in order to win an election, no problem. Just ask Colson to get it done, and don't ask for any of the details. Plausible deniability is always best for a president. After all, you need power to help other people, right? So what is the big deal about cutting corners to get it?

The trouble is, wrong is wrong, and the ends do not justify the means. When Colson helped Richard Nixon regain the presidency in 1972, it should have been the height of his career, but it wasn't. Despite having the thanks of the president of the United States of America for his faithful service, Charles Colson was empty inside. He didn't need power, money, and notoriety—he needed Jesus.

The story of Chuck Colson is a Paul story in modern times. Chuck met Jesus while working in the "dirty tricks" department for Richard Nixon—that's when he realized everything had to change. There would be no more lying. There would be no avoiding jail, even though he was never actually charged with anything that had to do with the Watergate break-ins. When accused of obstruction of justice in an unrelated case, Colson pleaded guilty and was sentenced to one to three years in prison. He ended up serving seven months and got out on good behavior. Where most would have put that behind them and moved on in life, Chuck Colson made it the defining crux of the rest of his life; he started a ministry to inmates—Prison Fellowship, now in 112 countries worldwide. All the proceeds from the twenty-three books he has written over the years since then—some of which have been best sellers—have all gone to support Prison Fellowship.

Charles Colson went from being a hatchet man who helped put a president in office, to an inmate, to one of the most prominent spokesmen for living life the Christian way the twentieth and twenty-first centuries have ever known. When Charles met Jesus back in his darkest days, he pledged to Him he would live for the truth from that day forward, no matter what it cost him. That integrity has literally touched a generation. Chuck Colson worked in the most influential building in the world, but it wasn't until he turned his back on that and pledged his life to God that he found his real influence. His book *Born Again* tells the honest and forthright story of what changed his life and consequently the lives of many others in succession. As I write this, Mr. Colson has just passed away at the age of eighty, after thirty-eight years of ministry. The legacy he leaves is one that will continue to touch lives far into the future.

What is the power of integrity? If you don't see it in the life of Charles Colson, then look at the life of Daniel. Daniel consecrated himself to God as a teenager and refused to eat meats from the king's table in order to honor his kosher heritage. Eating only vegetables, God made him and his three best friends, Shadrach, Meshach, and Abednego, shine above all the others. Daniel prayed three times a day looking toward where his home of Jerusalem had once stood and refused to honor any God except Jehovah. Because of his dedication to prayer and seeking God, when no one else in the kingdom could decipher the king's dream, Daniel could. Daniel is the only man mentioned in the Bible of whom nothing negative is recorded, other than Jesus. His notoriety for his dedication to God and his integrity was so famous among the other Jews that his contemporary Ezekiel, who was some years older than Daniel, compared Daniel's authority with God in prayer to that of Noah and Job:

> "Even though Noah, Daniel, and Job were in it, as I live," says the Lord GOD, "they would deliver neither son nor daughter; they would deliver only themselves by their righteousness."
> —EZEKIEL 14:20

The remarkable thing about this passage is that while Noah and Job had been heroes of the faith for generations, Daniel was only in his early thirties when this was written, years before his experience in the lions' den. Daniel's integrity was so great, he was mentioned among some of the greatest legends of the faith by God while he was still a relatively young man.

What was the reward of such integrity? As we have already discussed, God revealed some of the most important and foundational prophecies for the future of Judaism to Daniel. Daniel was the greatest of the Old Testament prophets, despite the fact that he worked in the government of an occupying power his entire life. Yet he was no collaborator. The Jewish people never doubted where his true allegiance lay, and the occupying kings valued him all the more for his devotion to his God.

Even when his life appeared to be on the line for his prayer habits, he refused to back away from them. Rather than have a question about where his true loyalties lay, he threw the windows of his prayer room open so that all could see him lay his requests before God rather than King Darius. When he was brought before the king, he told the whole truth and nothing but the truth. Then when he was thrown to the lions, God intervened and protected him—something that did not happen when his accusers got the same sentence. Daniel had integrity like no other person mentioned in the Bible except Jesus, and his deliverance and favor with God because of it was also like no other.

What evil does never lasts. What integrity builds remains forever.

Truth Always Rises to the Top

While we associate the word *integrity* with honesty, character, and unwavering adherence to a moral code of ethics, it is also used as a measure of uniformity and pureness. We talk about the integrity of steel as a measure of its strength or the integrity of a sample taken from something to see how untainted and trustworthy it is. We talk about the integrity of a structure when testing its soundness and resilience. I think all of these apply when we speak of having integrity before God.

It doesn't matter how good you look to people at church or at work. It doesn't matter what your reputation in your community is or if you have a small fortune in the bank. It doesn't matter if you show up at every prayer meeting and spend every hour of your church's twenty-four-hour prayer vigil on your face before God weeping. The only way to have true integrity is if you have integrity in your personal prayer closet before God. It is not about being seen by others or about what others think; it is about what God thinks and how much He trusts you with what He is doing on the earth. When something is about to happen, whom can He trust to tell about it so they will pray it through? Whom will He go to who will stand in the gap for that missionary in the field, that community about to be hit by a tornado, that pastor contemplating divorce, or that child about to be the victim of gang violence?

As Jesus put it:

> When you pray, you shall not be like the hypocrites. For they love to pray standing in the synagogues and on the corners of the streets, that they may be seen by men. Assuredly, I say to you, they have their reward. But you, when you pray, go into your room, and when you have shut your door, pray to your Father who is in the secret place; and your Father who sees in secret will reward you openly. And when you pray, do not use vain repetitions as the heathen do. For they think that they will be heard for their many words.
>
> —MATTHEW 6:5–7

Now, I am not bashing 24/7 prayer rooms—I think those are awesome and that we need more of them the world 'round—but if your only prayer is in front of other people, then I question your devotion to prayer and the integrity of your relationship with God. If Jesus is our *Lord* and Savior, how is it we do anything during that day without first checking in with Him?

If you read the stories of the great generals of prayer of the past, you will begin to see some patterns. One of the most important is that they didn't fit in prayer around their schedule of activities and speaking engagements; they fit in their activities and engagements around their prayer times. As Stephen Covey advocates, you have to put the "big rocks"—the most important things—onto your calendar first, or all of the little distractions and "urgent" matters of your day will not leave room for doing what is important. Prayer—or more simply put, "meeting with our Lord"—must be first place in everything we do if we are to know His plan, be free of worldly and earthly burdens, and have His wisdom in every matter. And I am not talking about a fleeting minute here and there, but an honest meeting time with God with your Bible open in front of you.

How that looks is totally up to you and God, however. If you have access to a 24/7 prayer room at your church or in your community, by all means spend some time praying corporately with others. There are myriads of different routines you can observe. Daniel prayed three times a day. You can practice something like "praying on the sevens," meaning you stop to pray at 7:00 a.m. and then at 7:00 p.m. Some feel they should "tithe their time" just as they tithe their income, so they spend two hours and twenty-four minutes a day in prayer and Scripture reading. At the same time, Smith Wigglesworth used to scoff at people who prayed more than twenty minutes at a time, but then when he thought about it, he noted that he never went more than twenty minutes without praying.

The apostle Paul advised us to "pray without ceasing" (1 Thess. 5:17) and to be "rejoicing in hope, patient in tribulation, continuing steadfastly [KJV, instant] in prayer" (Rom. 12:12). This seems to suggest we have a constant dialogue going on with God and that the best time to pray for anything is the "instant" the need is presented to us. I think this also suggests we need to avoid the Christianism, "I'll pray for you," and replace it with, "Let's pray now."

I am not trying to strap some burden on you with a legalistic pronouncement on how long or often you should pray each day. I spent years struggling to put prayer in its proper place in my life and still have days that try to crowd it out. What I am saying, though, is unless we make it a priority, we will never get the downloads from heaven that we need to fulfill our purposes on the earth. That will likely mean—as it did for me—spending a lot of time at the edge of eternity calling out into what feels like a void, banging on heaven's gate and feeling like no one is home. But the way things seem and the way they actually are, are two different things. As Scripture tells us:

> As you do not know what is the way of the
> wind,
> Or how the bones grow in the womb of her
> who is with child,
> So you do not know the works of God who
> makes everything.
> —ECCLESIASTES 11:5

In other words, when you plant a seed in the ground, you do not know what is happening with it until it pushes through the soil. There will be days and even weeks you might think nothing is happening at all, but it is growing and sprouting and getting ready to bear fruit. Prayer is the same way. What we do in secret may even be secret from us for a time, but when it manifests and sprouts, God will be glorified in it before all men.

When we sit at the awards ceremony of the marriage supper of the Lamb, we will be amazed that the biggest awards will not go to the televangelists and big-name ministers we all know and flock to hear. It will be to the widow who went into her room to pray each night for a church to be planted or the unknown janitor who laid his hands on every desk and child's locker, praying for a blessing on whoever touched it. God's heroes are not like our heroes— they are the ones who are most like Jesus. And what is Jesus doing right now? He is at the right hand of the Father interceding for us. If we want to be like Him, then prayer needs to be a central focus of our lives—just as it is the central focus of His now.

ALL THAT PERTAINS TO LIFE AND GODLINESS

In his second letter to the church at large, Peter wrote:

> Grace and peace be multiplied to you in the knowledge of God and of Jesus our Lord, as His divine power has given to us all things that pertain to life and godliness, through the knowledge of Him who called us by glory

> and virtue, by which have been given to us exceedingly great and precious promises, that through these you may be partakers of the divine nature, having escaped the corruption that is in the world through lust.
>
> —2 Peter 1:2–4

Peter's words here echo the purpose and petitions of Paul's first prayer in the Book of Ephesians. Through the knowledge of God we will receive all things needed for life and godliness—god-like-ness, if you will. Or in other words, being more like Jesus; ushering more of the kingdom of heaven onto this earth; fighting for the same justice Christians throughout history have been fighting for in establishing each generation. We have exceedingly great and precious promises that have been given to us so that we can live by the divine nature God has put into everyone who believes Jesus died for his or her sins and was raised back to life—that we would live by the fullness of the Holy Spirit seeded into us as a down payment on all God plans to do in, through, and for us. (See Ephesians 1:13–14.)

How is this to come about? To understand, we need to read further into what Peter wrote in this passage:

But also for this very reason, giving all diligence, add to your faith virtue, to virtue knowledge, to knowledge self-control, to self-control perseverance, to perseverance godliness, to godliness brotherly kindness, and to brotherly kindness love. For if these things are yours and abound, you will be neither barren nor unfruitful in the knowledge of our Lord Jesus Christ. For he who lacks these things is shortsighted, even to blindness, and has forgotten that he was cleansed from his old sins. Therefore, brethren, be even more diligent to make your call and election sure, for if you do these things you will never stumble; for so an entrance will be supplied to you abundantly into the everlasting kingdom of our Lord and Savior Jesus Christ.

—2 PETER 1:5–11

How would you like to never stumble in the call of God on your life? Peter gives us the key here: add to faith virtue (moral strength), add to virtue knowledge of God in your fields of study and in your occupations, add to knowledge self-discipline, add to self-discipline perseverance, add to perseverance kindness born out of brotherly love, and add to brotherly kindness the God-kind of love that never gives up, never gives in, never wavers, and never fails. (See 1 Corinthians 13:4–8.)

For us to live this kind of life, prayer must be at the center of all we do, for all of these are born out of prayer. When the kingdom of heaven and the kingdom of this world clash, it will be those who have heard from heaven that will supply the strategies to victory. It will be those with the most integrous—pure, honest, sound, strong, untainted, and stable—prayer lives that arise with the answers and the conviction to see the fight to its proper finish.

Be strong in the power of prayer. Be strong in the wisdom and might of God. Be exactly who He has called you to be right where you are today. The future of the kingdom is counting on you. There are others out there—future generations—who are counting on you. God is counting on you. You are the expression of Him on the earth "in which he speaks and acts, by which he fills everything with his presence" (Eph. 1:22–23, The MESSAGE).

Be the answer the world needs today by putting prayer at the center of your calendar and at the top of your to-do list. The life you will experience when you do this will be "exceedingly abundantly above all that we can ask or think" (Eph. 3:20).

Appendix A

ATOMIC POWER *of* PRAYER

TAKE THE THIRTY-DAY challenge. Pray this prayer aloud daily for thirty days. Gather a small or large group of individuals who will agree to pray with you. Covenant thereafter to pray consistently until you see positive change within your communities and nations. Lift your voice and unleash the atomic power of prayer.

Dear God:

- I arise today through the mighty strength of Your sovereignty, grace, divinity, and the knowledge that I was born within this generation to contribute something significant.

- I am not here by accident.

- You have placed me here to fulfill Your purpose.

- You have called me to be a world-class, moral, and ethical leader within my sphere of influence.

- I commit to bear Your light as an agent of change in a world of darkness.

- No one will meet me and not be positively impacted.

- I will responsibly utilize the gifts You have given me to be a blessing to my family, community, and nation.

- I arise today through the strength of Christ, demonstrated by His birth, burial, resurrection, and intercession.

- Shield me today against persecution and false accusation, against seduction, temptation, compromise, falsehood, slander, greed, discouragement, sabotage, accidents, death threats, mishaps, and manipulations so that there may come to me opportunities to become a better person.

- Let Your Spirit be with me, before me, behind me, in me, beneath me, above

me, on my right, on my left, when I
sit down, when I arise, when I speak,
in my business dealings, negotiations,
communications, crossing borders,
and when I retire for the night.

+ Let favor be in the heart of every man
who thinks of me, interacts with me,
and works with me.

+ Let truth be in the mouth of
everyone who speaks of and with me.

+ Let honor and high esteem be in
every eye that sees me.

+ Let good news and incredible reports
of my success and prosperity fill the
ears of everyone that hears of me.

+ According to Joshua 1:8, Philippians
4:8, and the laws that govern
attaining a conditioned and positive
mind-set, undergird me as I commit
to memorizing and repeating this
declaration aloud at least once a day.

+ Empower me to extract wisdom
from Your Word with full faith and

assurance that it will gradually influence my thoughts and actions until my life epitomizes the Word.

+ Help me to maintain a place amongst the great, powerful, influential, and affluent as a thought leader to the glory of God and the betterment of humanity.

+ I arise today in faith that You hear and answer prayer.

Father:

+ I thank You for boundless energy and rock-solid faith.

+ Thank You for giving me an overriding sense of peace, love, mercy, favor, and the absolute assurance that You are in control.

Since my times are in Your hand, I decree and declare that this year:

+ Is pregnant with purpose, promise, strategic encounters, wonderful surprises, and supernatural breakthroughs.

+ The best of my todays will become the worst of my tomorrows.

+ The pain of yesterday will never appear again in my tomorrow.

Father:

+ Let me forever live under an open heaven.

+ Grant me strategies for a prosperous and successful living.

Help me to:

+ Pray more.

+ Praise more.

+ Give more.

+ Believe more.

+ Hope more.

I decree that:

+ My mind is filled with the knowledge of my true identity.

- I am empowered to accomplish that which I was born to do and to live authentically.

- I become all that I was born to be.

- My destiny is in sync with Your perfect will.

- My vision is clear.

- My mission is unobstructed.

- My intentions and motives are pure.

- My relationships are healthy.

- All of my needs are supplied according to Your riches in glory.

- I am an influencer.

- I leave a legacy for the next generation.

- I live in a prosperous, healthy environment.

- You prosper the works of my hands.

- Everything I touch will turn into prophetic gold.

- My life reflects the shimmer of Your glory and divinity.

- My life, family, and friends are blessed with health and goodness.

- Joy, peace, prosperity, and success are as abundant as the stars at night.

- Mutually beneficial relationships, favor, affluence, influence, happiness, support, beauty, purpose, direction, and abundant living are my constant companions.

- I am unconditionally loved, celebrated, revered, appreciated, and honored beyond measure and all human comprehension.

- The fruit and gifts of the Spirit characterize my life.

- My life is characterized by righteousness and holiness.

- I make a difference in this world.

+ I have the courage to walk out my convictions and impact my spheres of influence.

+ I am a mover and shaker and history maker for Christ.

+ I recall my past as a testimony without the accompanied pain.

+ With the help of my God, I am granted quantum progress and divine acceleration.

I decree and declare:

+ My good name and good works will be memorialized to the glory of God.

+ My children fulfill their purpose and maximize their potential.

+ They have favor with God and man.

+ My creations, inventions, products, goods, and service are in high demand globally.

+ I am divinely positioned in a place that gives me a comparative advantage and competitive edge.

- My life and work are characterized by excellence, integrity, credibility, and honesty.

- My goals are achievable.

- My blessings, like the stars, are too numerous to count.

- Health and wealth walk with me, hand in hand.

- My victories are as abundant as the grains of sand.

- Lack and struggle are distant memories of the past.

- My enemies are subdued.

- I am fruitful in all my endeavors.

- I am granted multiple streams of income.

- I navigate these streams with an anointing that gives me business savvy.

- Abundant wealth is transferred into my hands and financial coffers, which include title deeds for commercial real estate and prime property.

- My income is greater than my expenditures.

- I have the disposal income to pay my government's taxes and tariffs.

- As a humanitarian, I have more than enough to give to those who can never repay the favor.

- I give a tenth of all my earnings to God so that there is no lack in His house.

- I also give to charitable and non-profit organizations whose focus is on helping the less fortunate, the orphan, widow, indigent, homeless, destitute, and helpless.

- My bank accounts are filled.

- My pocketbook never runs dry.

- Daily compounding interest favors my investments.

- My network and net worth increase profoundly.

- I am resourceful.

+ Everything I need is available to me as and when needed.

+ Blessings come upon me and overtake me.

+ My success confounds my critics and overwhelms my enemies.

+ My success convinces them that Jehovah God is the true and living God.

+ God releases divine angelic escorts to safely lead me into a goodly place where the lines of conviction are drawn in the sands of ethics and morality.

I decree and declare:

+ My head will never lack fresh oil.

+ My ears will forever be filled with good news.

+ My mouth is filled with spontaneous praise.

+ My hands never lack productivity.

+ My mind is filled with witty million-dollar ideas and creative billion-dollar inventions that positively impact the trajectory of humanity.

- My spirit is filled with God's abundant and divine presence.

- My soul is filled with joy and peace.

- My heart is filled with courage.

- My feet are free from obstructions.

- The light of God's Word illuminates my path.

- By its principles I blaze new trails and defy the status quo.

- By it I discover new horizons within my discipline, industry, profession, and chosen field.

- Abundant wealth, riches, music, and laughter fill my home.

- My every action and activity is synchronized and syncopated to heaven's rhythm.

- I live my life with integrity, morality, and credibility.

+ I conduct my business and financial affairs with ethics.

I decree and declare that:

+ My neighborhood and community are free from violence and criminal activities and that every evil work is mitigated and destroyed.

+ The spiritual, economic, social, and political climates shift and take a turn for the best.

+ The atmosphere within my community and nation is filled with the glory of God—an atmosphere conducive for businesses, ministries, agencies, institutions, educational and political systems, relationships, loved ones, and ideas to thrive.

+ My nation is characterized by a culture of empowerment.

Father:

+ Heal our land of civil unrest, ethnic cleansing, human trafficking, illegal countermands, pandemic disease, homelessness, illiteracy, and every evil work.

+ Cause economic and financial tides to turn in our favor.

+ Increase our GDP and GNP.

I decree and declare that:

+ The plans and purpose of God prevail within our communities and nations.

+ Our leadership, heads of state, government leaders, civil servants, decision makers, and political/moral leaders are blessed and corruption free.

Father:

+ Remove those who are driven by self-serving motivations and aspirations, and replace them with true and authentic servant-leaders.

I decree and declare that:

+ We experience supernatural increase.

+ We embrace the true wealth of nations.

- Our communities and nations experience economic growth, restoration, productivity, health, and hope.

- Our institutions, government, communities, and corporations are filled with moral, ethical, and visionary leadership.

- As a contributing member of our global village, I commit to do my part by rising up and taking a stand against violence, criminal activities, human rights violations, and social injustice and or/join others in mitigating, ameliorating, and eradicating the same.

Father:

- Show me the cause that I am assigned to champion.

- Give me the courage to rally others around plausible goals for nation-building, social reconstruction, community development, spiritual renewal, economic empowerment, policy-making, political enfranchisement, and educational reformation.

I decree that:

- We as responsible citizens will continue to raise the bar and push the envelope relative to fulfilling our spiritual and social contracts with the world and its communities.

- If I owe a debt to society, I will repay it.

Father:

- Allow us to live true to our core values and the Christian principles of Christ in the marketplace.

I decree and declare:

- I am the head and not the tail.

- That I will forever be first and not last.

- That I will forever be above only and not beneath.

- I live a humble life of gratitude and thanksgiving knowing that He who has begun this good work will complete it.

I seal this prayer in Jesus name. Amen.

Appendix B

"*In* CHRIST" SCRIPTURES

Being justified freely by His grace through the redemption that is in Christ Jesus.

—ROMANS 3:24

There is therefore now no condemnation to those who are in Christ Jesus, who do not walk according to the flesh, but according to the Spirit.

—ROMANS 8:1

For the law of the Spirit of life in Christ Jesus has made me free from the law of sin and death.

—ROMANS 8:2

For I am persuaded that neither death nor life, nor angels nor principalities nor powers, nor things present nor things to come, nor height nor depth, nor any other created thing, shall be able to separate us from the love of God which is in Christ Jesus our Lord.

—ROMANS 8:38–39

So we, being many, are one body in Christ, and individually members of one another.

—Romans 12:5

To the church of God which is at Corinth, to those who are sanctified in Christ Jesus, called to be saints, with all who in every place call on the name of Jesus Christ our Lord, both theirs and ours.

—1 Corinthians 1:2

But of Him you are in Christ Jesus, who became for us wisdom from God—and righteousness and sanctification and redemption.

—1 Corinthians 1:30

For as in Adam all die, even so in Christ all shall be made alive.

—1 Corinthians 15:22

Now He who establishes us with you in Christ and has anointed us is God.

—2 Corinthians 1:21

Now thanks be to God who always leads us in triumph in Christ, and through us diffuses the fragrance of His knowledge in every place.

—2 Corinthians 2:14

But their minds were blinded. For until this day the same veil remains unlifted in the reading of the Old Testament, because the veil is taken away in Christ.

—2 CORINTHIANS 3:14

Therefore, if anyone is in Christ, he is a new creation; old things have passed away; behold, all things have become new.

—2 CORINTHIANS 5:17

That is, that God was in Christ reconciling the world to Himself, not imputing their trespasses to them, and has committed to us the word of reconciliation.

—2 CORINTHIANS 5:19

But I fear, lest somehow, as the serpent deceived Eve by his craftiness, so your minds may be corrupted from the simplicity that is in Christ.

—2 CORINTHIANS 11:3

And this occurred because of false brethren secretly brought in (who came in by stealth to spy out our liberty which we have in Christ Jesus, that they might bring us into bondage).

—GALATIANS 2:4

And this I say, that the law, which was four hundred and thirty years later, cannot annul the covenant that was confirmed before by God in Christ, that it should make the promise of no effect.

—GALATIANS 3:17

For you are all sons [and daughters] of God through faith in Christ Jesus.

—GALATIANS 3:26

There is neither Jew nor Greek, there is neither slave nor free, there is neither male nor female; for you are all one in Christ Jesus.

—GALATIANS 3:28

For in Christ Jesus neither circumcision nor uncircumcision avails anything, but faith working through love.

—GALATIANS 5:6

For in Christ Jesus neither circumcision nor uncircumcision avails anything, but a new creation.

—GALATIANS 6:15

Blessed be the God and Father of our Lord Jesus Christ, who has blessed us with every spiritual blessing in the heavenly places in Christ.

—EPHESIANS 1:3

That in the dispensation of the fullness of the times He might gather together in one all things in Christ, both which are in heaven and which are on earth—in Him.

—EPHESIANS 1:10

In Him also we have obtained an inheritance, being predestined according to the purpose of Him who works all things according to the counsel of His will, that we who first trusted in Christ should be to the praise of His glory.

—EPHESIANS 1:11–12

In Him you also trusted, after you heard the word of truth, the gospel of your salvation; in whom also, having believed, you were sealed with the Holy Spirit of promise.

—EPHESIANS 1:13

And raised us up together, and made us sit together in the heavenly places in Christ Jesus.

—EPHESIANS 2:6

For we are His workmanship, created in Christ Jesus for good works, which God prepared beforehand that we should walk in them.

—Ephesians 2:10

But now in Christ Jesus you who once were far off have been brought near by the blood of Christ.

—Ephesians 2:13

That the Gentiles should be fellow heirs, of the same body, and partakers of His promise in Christ through the gospel.

—Ephesians 3:6

For we are the circumcision, who worship God in the Spirit, rejoice in Christ Jesus, and have no confidence in the flesh.

—Philippians 3:3

I press toward the goal for the prize of the upward call of God in Christ Jesus.

—Philippians 3:14

In everything give thanks; for this is the will of God in Christ Jesus for you.

—1 Thessalonians 5:18

And the grace of our Lord was exceedingly abundant, with faith and love which are in Christ Jesus.

—1 TIMOTHY 1:14

For those who have served well as deacons obtain for themselves a good standing and great boldness in the faith which is in Christ Jesus.

—1 TIMOTHY 3:13

Paul, an apostle of Jesus Christ by the will of God, according to the promise of life which is in Christ Jesus.

—2 TIMOTHY 1:1

Who has saved us and called us with a holy calling, not according to our works, but according to His own purpose and grace which was given to us in Christ Jesus before time began.

—2 TIMOTHY 1:9

Hold fast the pattern of sound words which you have heard from me, in faith and love which are in Christ Jesus.

—2 TIMOTHY 1:13

You therefore, my son, be strong in the grace that is in Christ Jesus.

—2 Timothy 2:1

Therefore I endure all things for the sake of the elect, that they also may obtain the salvation which is in Christ Jesus with eternal glory.

—2 Timothy 2:10

I thank my God, making mention of you always in my prayers, hearing of your love and faith which you have toward the Lord Jesus and toward all the saints, that the sharing of your faith may become effective by the acknowledgment of every good thing which is in you in Christ Jesus.

—Philemon 4–6

Having a good conscience, that when they defame you as evildoers, those who revile your good conduct in Christ may be ashamed.

—1 Peter 3:16

"Because of [by, through] Me [Jesus]"

Blessed is he who is not offended because of Me.

—Matthew 11:6

As the living Father sent Me, and I live because of the Father, so he who feeds on Me will live because of Me.

—John 6:57

I am the door. If anyone enters by Me, he will be saved, and will go in and out and find pasture.

—John 10:9

I am the way, the truth, and the life. No one comes to the Father except through Me.

—John 14:6

A little while longer and the world will see Me no more, but you will see Me. Because I live, you will live also.

—John 14:19

"In Me [Jesus]"

At that day you will know that I am in My Father, and you in Me, and I in you.

—John 14:20

Abide in Me, and I in you. As the branch cannot bear fruit of itself, unless it abides in the vine, neither can you, unless you abide in Me. I am the vine, you are the branches. He who abides in Me, and I in him, bears much fruit; for without Me you can do nothing. If anyone does not abide in Me, he is cast out as a branch and is withered; and they gather them and throw them into the fire, and they are burned. If you abide in Me, and My words abide in you, you will ask what you desire, and it shall be done for you.

—JOHN 15:4–7

These things I have spoken to you, that in Me you may have peace. In the world you will have tribulation; but be of good cheer, I have overcome the world.

—JOHN 16:33

NOTES

PART ONE
PRAYER FROM THE STRONGHOLD

1. E. M. Bounds, *Power Through Prayer* (New York: Cosimo, Inc., 2007, orig. published in 1906), 45.

CHAPTER 2
BATTLE STATIONS!

1. Adapted from 1 Kings 18:20–39. Text within quote marks and Elijah's prayer have been quoted directly from the Scriptures.

CHAPTER 3
SYNCING HEART AND PRACTICE

1. E. G. Carre, ed., *Praying Hyde: The Life Story of John Hyde* (Orlando, FL: Bridge Logos, 1982), 25.

CHAPTER 4
"FOR SUCH A TIME AS THIS"

1. For a more detailed explanation of these prophecies and how they are reflected in today's headlines, I urge you to read Michael D. Evan's book *The Final Generation* (Bedford, TX: Timeworthy Books, 2012).

2. Cornel West, *Brother West: Living and Loving Out Loud* (New York: Hay House, 2009), 232.

Part Two
Prayer on the Battlefronts

1. Andrew Murray, *With Christ in the School of Prayer* (n.p.: Wilder Publications, 2008), 134.

Chapter 5
Revolutionary Empowerment

1. "Vital Voices: The Story of Kakenya," YouTube. com, July 13, 2010, http://youtube.com/bwjv78L6BCk (accessed May 15, 2012).

Chapter 6
Delivering the Captives

1. Murray, *With Christ in the School of Prayer*, 28.
2. Shelley Hundley, *A Cry for Justice* (Lake Mary, FL: Charisma House, 2011), 31.
3. Ibid., 58–59.
4. Ibid., 63.

Chapter 7
Radical Economics

1. George Müller, *Answers to Prayer* (n.p.: ReadaClassic.com, 2010), 8.

Chapter 8
In Step With the Spirit

1. As quoted in Harold Chadwick, *How to Be Filled With Spiritual Power: Based on the Ministry of John G. Lake* (n.p.: ReadHowYouWant.com, n.d.).